INSTANT

EUROPEAN
HISTORY

EUROPEAN

HISTORY

FROM THE FRENCH REVOLUTION
TO THE COLD WAR

BY ROBERT P. LIBBON

A Byron Preiss Book

FAWCETT BOOKS • NEW YORK

CONTENTS

LIST OF MAPS

INTRODUCTION

A dmit it—your study of European history has been limited to watching a few World Cup games. You live in constant fear that someone's going to ask you what the difference is between Holland and the Netherlands. As far as you're concerned, "Holy Roman Empire" is something Robin used to say to Batman. Who can blame you? What is European history anyway but a series of names, dates, wars, and fifty kings named Louis? You have a hard enough time with those Adams presidents.

Relax. History isn't an endless parade of colorless rulers, faceless politicians, and meaningless dates. It's ambitious people with grand designs: Prince Otto von Bismarck, who forged a German empire only to have his emperor lead it into a disastrous world war; and Emperor Napoleon Bonaparte, who discovered that *The Road to Moscow* wasn't a comedy but a military version of *Ishtar*. It's about the English romantic poet Lord Byron, who died at 36 fighting for Greek independence, and David Livingstone, the Scottish explorer who left his heart not in San Francisco but in Africa. (When he died in Zambia, his pals planted his heart in the ground; the rest of him is buried at Westminster Abbey). These aren't just names that might be on the test, but actual people doing their best to muddle through like the rest of us. And none of *them* had the Discovery Channel to help them figure out who was supposed to win at Sebastopol (you'll have to wait until Chapter 2).

Instant European History guides you through the important events, movements, and trends of the last few centuries—without losing sight of the fact that behind every important movement is a human face asking the question: *Hey, what the heck happened?*

HOW THIS BOOK IS ORGANIZED

It doesn't get any simpler than this: At the beginning of each chapter you get a concise description of what the chapter is about—along with a shopping list of significant events and, as an extra added attraction, a "Who's Who" of important figures for the period. At the end of each chapter, you'll find a summary of what you've just read, in case you've already forgotten.

In between, as a bonus, you get the actual chapter, which provides a few details about the important people, places, events, and big-time ideas of the day. Along the way there are interesting sidebars to keep you going. The sidebars alone will supply you with enough information to ace the European History category on "Jeopardy", which after all is the one true sign of scholarship in the United States. (No, there is no *Instant Potpourri.*) Here's a preview of what's to come:

Chapter 1: Absolutism, Enlightenment, Revolution, and Empire (1700–1815) kicks off our story in 1700 with a French king named Louis XIV and concludes in 1815 with a French emperor named Napoleon. In between: a minor disturbance known as the French Revolution.

Chapter 2: Political Reaction and Industrial Development (1815–1870) is the play-by-play of the political struggles between 1815 and 1870—when students skipped school to build barricades and the French installed a revolving door in the royal palace—played out against the steamy backdrop of the Industrial Revolution.

Chapter 3: National Competition and Overseas Expansion (1870–1914) finds the major European powers, led by a unified German Empire, acting like bullies across the globe and braggarts at home. A continent-wide arms race turns Europe into a time bomb—with the clock set at 1914.

Chapter 4: A Half Century of Wars (1914–1945) begins with "the war to end all wars," rolls through a brief time-out for rearmament, and concludes as the Allied victory in World War II leads not to peace but to Cold War.

That's what lies ahead. But before we begin, here's a brief recap of what you've missed so far (Europe didn't spring into existence in 1700, you know). For some added drama, tilt the page away from you while you read this section—that way it looks like the opening to the *Star Wars* movies.

THE STORY SO FAR . . .

Although Europe's "modern age" began in the sixteenth century, it took two centuries of growing pains to forge the systems that we recognize as modern:

- a state system driven by secular concerns (not religious dogma);
- a growing mercantilist system of trade, banking, and colonization;
- a scientific system of natural laws that includes the philosophy of human affairs.

For the genesis of these systems we have to look back to the sixteenth century, when three broad movements transformed the relationship between individuals and their world.

EXPANSION

Intrepid explorers (Italy's Christopher Columbus, Portugal's Ferdinand Magellan and Vasco da Gama) sailing to distant shores made a wonderful discovery in the sixteenth century: The world was full of unclaimed, unexplored territory replete with gold, silver, and all kinds of new food. Better still was the discovery that this valuable stuff belonged to people who were really easy to conquer—either by the use of arms or the importation of European diseases that ravaged native populations.

The proceeds of exploration (a blanket term covering not just exploring but also claiming, converting, slaving, pillaging, and killing) spurred the building of new political states (the Spain of Ferdinand and Isabella, the England of Queen Elizabeth), the emergence of modern banking practices, the growth of cities, and a dramatic increase in military and naval activities. Every major power had a navy, and most states founded colonies—so that much of Africa, the Americas, and Asia were remapped to reflect European presence.

The biggest winners in expansion's first round were Spain and England; it helped that they had ample coastlines from which to launch ships. (Quick—name a Swiss explorer.)

THE RENAISSANCE

The Renaissance was a sweeping artistic and philosophical movement that not only celebrated human form and potential but also supplied names for the Teenage Mutant Ninja Turtles. It broke with traditional disdain for all things classical in its celebration of Roman and Greek antiquity and in its focus on earthly pursuits rather than heavenly visions. Beginning in the newly prosperous Italian city-states of the late fourteenth century, the Renaissance had spread through most of Western Europe by the end of the sixteenth century.

The Renaissance was bankrolled by powerful merchant families like the Medicis and Sforzas, who as patrons of the arts and sciences commissioned works by artists such as Leonardo da Vinci, Titian, Botticelli, and Donatello. This sudden burst of lay interest in philosophy, science, and art (subjects which, during the Middle Ages, had been the bailiwick of the Church) gave the Renaissance a distinctly secular tilt. Michelangelo's marble statue *David* (1501–1504), a naturalistic portrait of human confidence and ability, is considered the epitome of the Renaissance.

THE REFORMATION

In 1517, Martin Luther (1483–1546), a priest as well as a professor at the University of Wittenberg, nailed his Ninety-Five Theses, or points of debate, to the church door of Wittenberg Castle. This sixteenth-century version of certified mail was a direct challenge to Church authority; Luther's theses attacked widespread Church abuse and corruption. In publicly airing the Church's dirty habits, Luther offended papal authority by assuming that he had the right to even question the Church. To make matters worse, it seemed Luther also had the wacky idea that he could better approach God through personal prayer rather than through Church sacrament. Indeed, according to Luther, the only thing anyone really needed to achieve salvation was a Bible. And since the invention of the printing press, *anybody* could get one of those. (Being able to read it was another matter.)

You can imagine how well this went over with the boys in the Vatican. Luther was hauled before the powers-that-be and told to change his mind. When he refused, they threw the Good Book at him. Excommunicated, he continued to advocate religious reform, with far-reaching results. The idea that papal authority and practice could be questioned, much less ignored, by an individual was a threat to those ruling powers closely allied to the papacy—the Kingdom of Spain and the Holy Roman Empire (then comprising present-day Germany, Austria, Switzerland, the Netherlands, and parts of France, Italy and Czechoslovakia). A religious matter (the individual's relationship to God) spilled into the political arena (the individual's relationship to authority), with predictably bloody results.

Dissatisfied nobles in the German principalities of Holy Roman Emperor Charles V (1500–1558) revolted in the Knights' War of 1522. Jealous peasants wanted their own war and got it—the Peasants' War of 1524–1526. King Philip II of Spain (1527–1598), a fanatic defender of the Catholic faith, was faced with Protestant revolt in the Netherlands throughout the second half of the sixteenth century. More telling was the fate of Philip's "Invincible Armada," the 130-ship fleet he sent against Protestant England in 1588. He had long suffered English attacks on his silver-bearing ships from America. When Elizabeth I executed her Catholic cousin, Mary, Queen of Scots, Philip lost his patience and sent his fleet to teach England a lesson. Unfortunately for Spain, that lesson was "How to Sink the Spanish Armada." English seamanship and bad weather combined to send about two-thirds of King Philip's navy to the ocean floor. England's long day as a great sea power began, while Spain would in the next century pass into a long dusk.

Religious wars continued into the seventeenth century. The Thirty Years' War (1618–1648) began in Prague when Protestants threw a couple of Catholic ministers out a window. (In those days this was considered a hostile act, not a club dance.) The ensuing war spread through the Continent, eventually drawing in the German principalities, Spain, the Holy Roman Empire, Sweden, Denmark, and France.

It was during this war that something curious happened. In 1635 Catholic France entered the war on the side of Protestant Sweden. She did so because Louis XIII, a member of the Bourbon dynasty, saw an opportunity to weaken the rival Hapsburg family, whose branches ruled both Spain and the Holy Roman Empire. By placing national interest above religious principle, France altered the nature of the war. Other participants followed suit, their political concerns also taking precedence over religion, heralding a long decline of religious influence in state affairs.

At the Peace of Westphalia (1648) France and Sweden came out on top; Spain and the Netherlands slipped out of the political mainstream. The Holy Roman Empire, although still a formidable force, lost its German principalities, making it more a dynastic Austrian state under Hapsburg rule than a Holy Roman Empire.

By the end of the seventeenth century, modern Europe had taken shape. The prevailing European state, now devoted to secular and national interests, was absolute monarchy: the unquestioned, unchecked power of a monarch who ruled by "divine right"—the principle that rulers derive their power directly from God. Consequently, their responsibility was either to God or to their consciences, certainly not to their subjects, who were expected to live and die with a minimum of fuss, pay taxes and fight wars, and trust in a glorious afterlife.

Best exemplified by the splendid personage of France's King Louis XIV (known as the "Sun King" because it takes too long to remember what XIV means), absolute monarchs held the reins of social, political, economic, and military power. This gave them the ability (if not necessarily the judgment) to dedicate the resources of the state to the increasingly expensive business of war.

Louis XIV's pervasive influence can be seen in two of the numerous works for which he is responsible: his magnificent palace at Versailles (begun in 1661) and the French Academy of Science (established 1666). Although the former remains a monument to absolutism, the latter has become a symbol of an intellectual movement that eventually threatened the very legitimacy of absolute rule. For just as power—not faith—had become the guiding principle of state by the end of the seventeenth century, so reason—not faith—had taken priority in science and philosophy. Where Martin Luther had placed personal worship above religious dogma, Galileo had put his faith in personal experimentation and observation, not Church doctrine. (Galileo, like Luther, was given the choice between renouncing his views and being excommunicated. He recanted, but later said he'd kept his fingers crossed.) In the seventeenth century, René Descartes (1596–1650) endorsed the notion that each of us can be a detached analytical observer (perhaps even a color commentator). And after Isaac Newton's (1642–1727) mechanistic analysis of the natural world, it was only a matter of time before someone began to analyze political structures with the same critical attitude. The resulting philosophy would finally produce a response to Louis XIV's famous line, "I am the State": *Says who?*

*   *   *

Heading into the eighteenth century, Europe was no longer a hotbed of religious conflict, but a collection of relatively coherent states looking to further their interests without too much trouble. (A thirty-year war was considered "trouble.") Disputes over colonial possessions, national borders, and dynastic successions had taken precedence over matters of faith; international affairs rested in the hands of diplomats, not popes. To better direct national affairs, rulers had unchecked authority over their realms. (The exception to the absolutist rule was England, where the Glorious Revolution of 1688 concluded a decades-long struggle between Parliament and the Stuart kings, replacing absolute monarchy with constitutional monarchy.) Absolute monarchs spent their days taxing and spending, regulating economic affairs, occasionally creating financial and moral scandals. (I *told* you this was modern Europe.)

Yet the mightiest state of them all—France—would be the first to fall.

EUROPEAN
HISTORY

CHAPTER 1

ABSOLUTISM, ENLIGHTENMENT, REVOLUTION, AND EMPIRE
(1700–1815)

YOU MUST REMEMBER THIS

Absolute monarchy—the concentration of power, by divine right, in the hands of a ruler—came under attack in the eighteenth century. Economic and political imbalance, coupled with a philosophical movement known as the Enlightenment, sparked the French Revolution—yet when the smoke had cleared, France had done away with a king (Louis XVI) only to put an emperor (Napoleon Bonaparte) in his place.

IMPORTANT EVENTS

★ England and Scotland joined to become Great Britain, 1707
★ Death of Louis XIV, 1715
★ Publication of Diderot's *Encyclopédie*, France, 1751–1765

★ The Seven Years' War, 1756–1763
★ Decade of the French Revolution, 1789–1799
★ Execution of Louis XVI, 1793
★ Napoleon seizes power, 1799
★ Battle of Waterloo, 1815

Absolutism got off to a good start in the eighteenth century. The lineup of absolute monarchs in the early 1700s included Russia's Peter the Great (1672–1725), whose fierce program of Westernization made Russia a major player in European affairs; Austria's Leopold I (1640–1705), who added Hungary to the Hapsburg empire; and Frederick I (1657–1713), first king of the newly independent kingdom of Prussia. In France under Louis XIV (1638–1715), the *ancient régime* (old order) of absolutism seemed especially entrenched.

But the legitimacy of the old order was already being undermined by the Enlightenment, a philosophical movement celebrating the power of reason. The prevailing order depended on blind trust in Church and State and a reliance on tradition and birth. Enlightenment thinkers like Voltaire, Diderot, and Rousseau, however, declared their faith in people's ability to understand and improve their world, to use reason and ability for their own betterment. Obviously, something had to give, and in France it did so cataclysmically. In 1789 the *ancient régime,* incapable of recognizing and correcting its irrelevance, was ruthlessly leveled. Louis XV's reported prediction, *"Après moi, le déluge,"* was more telling then he could have imagined. Seventy-five years after Louis XIV died of natural causes, Louis XVI was guillotined; barely a century after Protestantism was outlawed in France, the Catholic Church found its property confiscated by a new, republican government. The era began with the Sun King (Louis XIV), who personified divine right

WHO'S WHO

Voltaire (1694–1778): Born François Arouet, one of the wittiest and sharpest social critics of his time; author of *Candide* (1759).

Adam Smith (1723–1790): A major figure in the Scottish Enlightenment; renowned as the author of *Wealth of Nations* (1776).

Jean-Jacques Rousseau (1712–1778): Political theorist whose *Social Contract* (1962) is a major work on the origins of state and society.

Denis Diderot (1713–1784): Writer, philosopher, and editor who battled censorship and risked imprisonment to publish the multivolume *Encyclopédie,* a monument of Enlightenment philosophy.

Maximilien Robespierre (1758–1794): Fanatic revolutionary who presided over the Reign of Terror.

Napoleon Bonaparte (1769–1821): French general and emperor who reached the height of his power without powerful height.

and absolute monarchy, and closed with the modern world's closest relative—an emperor who personified human potential and supreme power.

TELL US ABOUT
OUR NEW CONTESTANTS

The seventeenth century had seen the emergence of France, Austria, and England as major European powers. Joining them at the start of the eighteenth century were two new players who owed their ascendancy to the efforts of vigorous rulers: Russia, under Peter the Great, and Prussia, under Frederick William I (1688–1740).

The basis for Prussia's emergence as a major power was its dedication to military strength. Whereas Frederick I had been an absolutist spendthrift, his son, Frederick William I, (1688–1740), disdained spectacle. Upon his succession in 1713, he undertook an intense program of domestic reform, streamlining the country's finances and beginning a military buildup that made Prussia a force to be reckoned with.

Peter the Great, czar (after 1682) of a country that spanned east and west, looked West for inspiration. In

Go West, young man: In 1697, Csar Peter the Great (1672–1725) toured Western Europe with a team of Russina diplomats. To avoid being constrained by official duties, he went incognito—a rather futile attempt at anonymity, given the well-known fact that the Csar, at 6'7", towered over everyone else in the Russian entourage.

1697 he made an extended tour of Western Europe, and evidently liked what he saw. Upon his return to Russia, he ordered the restructuring of his country along Western lines. The military was revamped to imitate Western armies, and a Russian navy was built. The establishment of a Russian Academy of Science followed proposals made by Leipzig's Gottfried Wilhelm von Leibniz (1646–1716), inventor of a system of calculus. Peter encouraged the emigration of technicians and artisans from the West, and he built a new capital on the Baltic Sea (after taking the territory from Sweden in 1703): St. Petersburg, Peter's "window to the West," became the royal residence in 1713. Through Peter's reorganization, Russia was not only able to displace Sweden as a Baltic power in the Great Northern War (1700–1721) but also began to figure in the balance of power in his beloved West.

THE BALANCE OF POWER

War was still everyone's favorite game in the eighteenth century, but the rules had changed. Since the middle of the seventeenth century, a state system had been emerging in Europe, a kind of five-member Friars' Club of European powers (France, Austria, Russia, Prussia, and England) that got together every so often to roast one of its members. The purpose of the system was to maintain relative parity among the five European powers, thus ensuring that no one of them became strong enough to dominate Europe. Instead of always trying to annihilate one another, the powers sought to keep a stable balance of power among themselves.

This meant simply that whenever one power threatened to tip the balance by becoming inordinately strong, the others would gang up and beat it back down. After a few lopsided battles, the loser would sue for peace, and a horde of diplomats would converge on a major city to hammer out a treaty while eating and drinking the town dry. There would be a few months of relative calm, until someone else tried to get out of line, and the whole business would start all over again. It was a nice, rational approach to international belligerence, and reflected the emerging belief that nations, as well as people, could determine their fate through the exercise of reason. To this end, states regularized the outfitting of armies, refined the exercise of diplomacy, and established royal arsenals. Foreign policy became the dominant concern of government in this century and has remained so in Europe to this day.

Now this state system didn't prevent war, of course—just made it tidier and less passionate and altogether less disruptive. People still got killed, but it was nothing personal—just another episode of "Truce or Consequences." Alliances were based on immediate expediency, not religious fervor or nationalistic zeal. The period's three wars of succession (also known as dynastic wars) are less important as events than as expressions of the state system, in which the balance of power was maintained through localized hostilities and temporary alliances. The War of the Spanish Succession (1701–1714) saw France's attempt to secure the Spanish throne thwarted by England, Prussia, and Austria; the War of Polish Succession (1733–1735) concerned the competition between France and Austria for Poland's throne; the War of the Austrian Succession (1740–1748) found Austria under attack by Prussia and her erstwhile ally France— when the dust had settled, Austria and France found themselves allied against Prussia and England. Everyone changed partners ("Okay, now I hate *you*") and went on with the dance.

THE ENGLISH AT HOME

Domestic politics in England reflected her geographic separation from the rest of Europe. While absolute monarchies on the Continent continued to turn a blind eye to reform, the English had already taken the "absolute" out of their monarchy in the previous century. They had executed one king (Charles I) in 1649, and thrown another out (his son, James II) in the Glorious Revolution of 1688 (so called because it peacefully handed the crown to William of Orange and Mary II, James II's Protestant daughter). All this confusion at the top served to establish the sovereignty of Parliament, which by 1707's Act of Union united Scotland and England to form the United Kingdom of Great Britain.

Parliament's Act of Settlement (1701) inadvertently maintained the growth of parliamentary influence, inasmuch as it handed the crown to a series of inattentive monarchs. The act, designed to keep the crown on Protestant heads, determined that upon Queen Anne's death (she had succeeded William and Mary in 1702) the succession would pass to the German Hanover line rather than to another member of the Stuart line. What was wrong with the Stuarts? With the notable exception of Queen Anne herself, they were Roman Catholic—which, in England, invariably meant popish, anti-Parliament, absolutist, intolerant, and just plain icky. George I of Hanover was the Protestant great-grandson of England's James I (sponsor of the King James Bible); giving George the crown secured the succession for his Protestant line.

For most of the eighteenth century, the Hanovers— kings in Great Britain and electors in Hanover (so called because Hanover was one of nine German principalities that elected the Holy Roman Emperor)— gave priority to their interests on the Continent. George I (1660–1727) came to the English throne in 1714, but never even bothered to learn English and spent a good deal of time in Hanover. Needless to say, he wasn't terribly popular with the Brits. His son, George II (1683–1760), became king in 1727 and like his father paid more attention to Germany than to Great Britain. It wasn't until George III (1738–1820) became king in 1760 that a Hanover ruler really concentrated on being king of Great Britain. He was in for a few surprises.

In the extended absences of George III's predecessors, the Whig party—the Parliamentary force behind the Glorious Revolution—had established various offices to help administrate the country. The staffing of these ministries had been overseen by Sir Robert Wal-

*King George III.
Great Britain's third
Hanoverian king
was the first to be
born in England.*

pole (1676–1745), the Whig leader whose commanding role made him the nation's "prime" minister (the
title itself, though widely used, didn't become official
until 1905). George III's zeal for directing national
policy brought him into conflict with the
independent-minded ministries, and only through
some fancy political footwork did he manage to select
ministers favorable to his views. One such minister was
Frederick North (1732–1792), who in twelve years as
prime minister was of invaluable assistance in pro-
voking the revolt and eventual loss of the English colonies in America. North resigned, and in 1783 George
appointed William Pitt (1759–1806) prime minister.

It was a fortunate move. The king, now suffering
from intermittent bouts of delirium, needed an able
minister, and Pitt was much more than that. Only 24
years old when he assumed the prime ministry, the
Bill Gates of his time instituted economic policies that

revitalized the country—just in time for another war with France.

GRUDGE MATCH

If there was one thing you could depend on during the eighteenth-century era of fair-weather friendships, it was that France and England were on opposite sides of any given conflict. Their rivalry intensified in this century and would be the major source of antagonism—both on the Continent and around the world—for the next hundred years. Their enmity found expression on North American soil in the French and Indian Wars, the last of which (1754–1763) was actu-

---

FREE-FOR-ALL . . . .

Overseas conflict between France and England was just one feature of the Seven Years' War (1756–1763), whose participants included Great Britain, the German principality of Hanover (naturally, since the Hanover line also ruled Great Britain), and Prussia on one side; and France, Austria, Russia, Sweden, and Spain on the other. In Europe, the Prussian army under King Frederick II (1712–1786) faced a coalition of Austrian, Russian, French, and Swedish forces. Aided by Russia's withdrawal in 1762 (the new czar, Peter III, was a big fan of Frederick), Prussia managed a stalemate against a formidable array of enemies—a military achievement that earned Frederick his familiar sobriquet: "the Great."

ally a component of the Seven Years' War (1756–1763) that saw France and England competing across three continents: Europe, America, and Asia.

In North America, France displayed a commendable respect for tradition by losing to the British, ceding her Canadian territories (so *that's* why they speak French in Quebec!) to England. In India, at the Battle of Plassey (1757), England ended France's hopes of establishing an empire there. It wasn't until allying herself with the colonies in the American Revolution that France managed a victory against the English. It

I'D LIKE A BIG MAC AND A DRIVER'S LICENSE, PLEASE

To understand how England's colonial interests complemented the interests of its merchant class, all you have to do is look at the English East India Company. Granted its charter in 1601 by Queen Elizabeth, and extended in perpetuity by James I, the East India Company was half corporation, half military force—and all business. Its charter granted it a legal monopoly on *all trade* in Asia, America, and Africa, giving the company the authority to oust not just foreign competitors but also native governments if necessary. (Imagine a combination of McDonald's and the United States Navy.) The Battle of Plassey did more than discourage French ambitions in India. It established the East India Company as the de facto rulers of the subcontinent.

For the next 175 years the company operated as a sanctioned arm of the English government while

I'D LIKE A BIG MAC AND A DRIVER'S LICENSE, PLEASE (*continued*)
....
generating tremendous private profit. Gradually, the British government weaned the company from its military and administrative roles and ended its sanctioned monopoly on trade. When the company was relieved of its military responsibilities in 1858, its military wing was absorbed by the British army.

was an expensive victory, for the cost of their participation played a significant role in the French Revolution.

The ongoing enmity between the two great powers is often seen as a conflict between representatives of two different eras. England had already redefined her monarchy's role (by cutting off Charles I's head) in the seventeenth century, altering her political structure to recognize the now-dominant merchant classes. The English song "Rule Britannia" implied rule by a trading class interested chiefly in profit, not power; gain, not glory. When it came time to pay the war's tremendous bill, England could look to the traders who had participated in the war and who had prospered by expansion. Although France remained the dominant military power on the Continent, her outdated political order excluded those whose help she needed to continue financing wars. Most notable among those excluded was the bourgeoisie—the middle class of merchants, bankers, lawyers, doctors, and manufacturers increasingly dissatisfied with the existing order known as the *ancien régime.*

OLD AND IN THE WAY

Ancien régime isn't French for "the good old days." Rather, it describes a political, social, and economic structure that pervaded Europe prior to the French Revolution. In the *ancien régime,* natural talent and ability, hard work and determination, had nothing to do with one's place in the world. You couldn't just call yourself "Duke," "Count," or "the noble formerly known as Prince." All that mattered was birth. Were you "to the manor born" or were you not? If you were of high birth, you automatically had the right to do nothing but dress up and hang around the palace, sniffing snuff and powdering your wig. It was a sweet life for the few born to this life of property and privilege—full of pomp, devoid of purpose. To be sure, there were exceptions to this rigid order. Voltaire made a good living and gained stature by his wit and writing. The Rothschild family ran banks in Vienna, Paris, and London—and eventually attained noble status. But for the most part, you picked the right parents or you didn't—and that was the end of the matter.

It hadn't always been this way. If the *régime* had been of no use at all, it would hardly have become *ancien.* This way of doing things had been established in medieval times and reflected that age's conception of distinct and divided social responsibility among three classes, called estates. The First Estate—the clergy—was responsible for the spiritual well-being of its community. The Second Estate—the aristocracy—was the class of nobility responsible for providing military support for the king. The Third Estate—the peasantry and later the bourgeoisie as well—was the overwhelming majority of the populace and was responsible for the production of goods.

CLERGY: THE FIRST ESTATE

In the *ancien régime,* the First Estate was a major player in state affairs. In contrast to the separation of Church and State that we take for granted today, at that time the Church was universally accepted as a pillar of the State. Through sermon and ceremony, the clergy—whose members included both commoners and aristocrats—reinforced the king's pretension to divine right. Ecclesiastical courts assisted in administration as well, overseeing marriages, births, and deaths. Two French cardinals, Richelieu (of *Three Musketeers* fame) and Mazarin, even served as foreign ministers.

The Church had good reason for its support of the status quo: real estate. Almost 10 percent of the country was occupied by monasteries, cathedrals, parish churches, and the like. Church possessions extended even to acres of valuable farmland. These holdings naturally made the clergy, like the monarchy, a conservative institution. Between the two, they provided the rationale for blind acceptance of authority in both secular and spiritual matters. The king, ruling "by the grace of God," was the arbiter of this world; the Church, arbiter of the next.

ARISTOCRACY:
THE SECOND ESTATE

In the Second Estate we find the courtiers with names like La Rochefoucauld-Liancourt hanging around ornate drawing rooms and laughing delicately into frilly sleeves. But these types were in the minority of the French aristocracy, numbering around a thousand out of 200,000 in the Second Estate. (France's total population was about 26 million.) The bulk of the aristocracy was scattered about the countryside, and its members were more inclined to wipe their noses on their sleeves than to laugh into them. In contrast to the palace hangers-on, many of these titled landowners had little wealth, despite their fine names. They had a reputation for profligacy and gluttony and often lived little better than the surrounding peasantry.

In addition to this geographical distinction, the aristocracy was divided in terms of origin. If you were of the "nobility of the sword," it meant that your family had earned its status by fighting on behalf of the king and you could wear your swords at court. If you were a member of the more recent "nobility of the robe," it meant that you'd managed to buy your way into a title, perhaps by purchasing a judicial office or performing some noncombative service for the monarchy. (Presumably you could wear your robe at court.) Charles de Secondat (1689–1755) was one of this group. His family, long in law, had been ennobled, and so he became Baron de Montesquieu. (It is as Montesquieu that Secondat is known for his 1748 political treatise *The Spirit of Laws,* which advocated a system of "checks and balances" between branches of government.) Still more recent were those whose great wealth and influence was recognized through the bestowing of a title.

. . . AND EVERYBODY ELSE: THE THIRD ESTATE

Everyone not in the First or Second Estates ended up in the Third—which, for a long time, simply meant the peasantry. In France, 80 percent of the population—21 out of 26 million—were peasants. As usual, they provided most of the work, most of the produce—and most of the taxes. Since the clergy was in the habit of receiving tithes, not paying out taxes, and the nobility had long forgotten how to fight, let alone work, it was left to the peasants to provide revenue for everyone. It hardly made a difference to them that a feudal obligation to their lord had, with time, become a strictly financial deal.

As property holders or tenant farmers, peasants were still in the same debt-ridden boat as before. They might be allowed to farm a few acres belonging to a local landowner in exchange for a hefty chunk of the produce, after which the king would insist upon his 20 or 30 percent. (Less than half of the peasantry owned land, and even those who did were often forced to work as laborers elsewhere to supplement what they managed to squeeze out of their small holdings.) This extortionate taxation left the peasant at the mercy of even the smallest swings in the agrarian economy. In good years most had to eke out a living on a day-to-day basis. In years of bad harvests shortages led to "bread riots" in the cities, as prices climbed far beyond the grasp of those who actually had produced the bread.

THE BOURGEOISIE

Over the years, another class joined the peasantry in the Third Estate: the bourgeoisie. As diplomacy and the state system made war more localized and less disruptive, commerce in European cities flourished. The markets were primarily in textiles (lace of Antwerp and Bruges, silk of Lyons, and wool exported from England through London) and consumable goods (tobacco, sugar, and rum of the New World, port and sherry of Portugal and Spain, fish from the coasts of the North Sea, and spices from the Far East). With this growth of urban commerce came a new class: the bourgeoisie, or "guys who live in bourgs." (*Bourg* was the French word for the fort or castle around which many cities developed.) This was the urban middle class whose lives revolved around production and trade, and whose currency was . . . well . . . *currency*. As the production and trade of goods blossomed, money supplanted barter as the principal medium of trade. The middle class controlled the flow of currency and profited from opportunities in the foreign exchange market. With this new wealth came new opportunity and prominence.

It was fashionable at the time to deride these upstarts—the *nouveau riche*—who dared think that money could raise them from their ignoble origins. This, in spite of the fact that the king himself was hardly above selling a title here or there for a little cash. The French playwright Moliére had already started the sniping in 1670 with his play *The Bourgeois Gentleman,* in which the title character asks a music instructor: "Do men of quality know music?" When told yes, he announces: "Then, I will learn it." To be sure, many of the bourgeoisie attempted to emulate that exclusive club, the Second Estate, by purchasing fine art *(Dogs Playing Poker),* creating ancestral lineages (the royal House of Pancakes), and adopting various trappings of nobility (gout). On the other hand many used commercial opportunity and success to establish their own clubs, a number of which survived the *ancien régime* itself. The Rothschilds, as we have seen, founded a banking dynasty. The English company founded by Josiah Wedgwood for the manufacture of fine pottery is in operation to this day.

Growing opportunities in commerce attracted both moralists and rascals. Speculation, cheating, double-crossing, and outright theft were rampant as those both earnest and cruel sought to make their fortunes (kind of like the New Hampshire primary). People flocked to the colonies to establish trading empires in tobacco, sugar, rum, and slaves. The most conspicuous of these colonial opportunists were English officials of the East India Company, dubbed "nabobs." The name is a corruption of *nawab,* the local word for a regional governor in eighteenth-century India. English officials displaced these native governors and used their offices to amass huge personal fortunes, with which they often built large estates when they returned to England. Nabob acquired such a negative connotation that two centuries later U.S. Vice President Spiro Agnew used it to attack critics of his administration, labeling them "nattering nabobs of negativism." (Okay, but what does *nattering* mean?)

The flip side of this opportunistic greed can be seen in someone like Benjamin Franklin, a self-made man who became rich enough at 40 to devote himself to science and writing. He represents not just the growing importance and potential of the bourgeoisie, but also the emerging belief that people could, through reason and ability, improve their condition. It was a radical thought, for it stood in direct opposition to the *ancien régime,* which was predicated on tradition and the accident of birth. As economic power passed from the farm to the city, from the propertied aristocracy and clergy to the urban middle class, it became obvious that the *ancien régime* had long outlived its relevance. Indeed, the rigid social, economic, and political order it represented became an obstruction to further progress. Clearly, a change in the prevailing order was needed. The Enlightenment provided the philosophical backbone for that change.

THE ENLIGHTENMENT

The ideas that emerged during the Enlightenment were more than illuminating. They were downright inspiring—for they represented a philosophy of reason, progress, and liberty. Imagine being told for years that your natural condition is misery and sin and that

your only hope for salvation lies in the next world—
and in order to secure *that,* you had to submit to the
will of the Church and State while you're here. (This
is easy for Chicago Cubs fans.) Then one day some
guy named Rousseau walks up to you and says: "You
know what? The institutions you bow and scrape before are actually keeping you from your natural, *right-
ful* place in the world. If you were only able to live
according to natural, rational law, you could learn
about the world, and master it. You would be happy."

AND YOU THINK THE *DEFICIT'S* BALLOONING?

The Enlightenment placed a premium on "better living through reason." Science was a noble pursuit,
but nobler still if it had a practical application. France's Montgolfier brothers, Jacques and Joseph, decided to make hot air practical. In 1783 they sent
up the first hot-air balloon. Later that year, they demonstrated their invention to Louis XVI and Marie Antoinette, using a few small animals as passengers.
(Yes, they got them back down.) The following year
another Frenchman, Jean Rozier, made the first
manned ascent in a balloon. And in 1785 Jean Pierre
Blanchard, with American John Jeffries, made the
first aerial crossing of the English Channel.

Blanchard is also credited with inventing the first
practical parachute, in 1785. In 1793 he claimed to
have made the first successful manned parachute descent. Oddly, no one has ever claimed credit for the
first *unsuccessful* manned parachute descent.

In a sense, the Enlightenment was a natural out-growth of Sir Isaac Newton's *Principia* (1687), which sought to describe nature by means of rational, consistent laws. Further discovery of these laws neces-sarily entailed exploration and classification: Swedish botanist Carolus Linnaeus (1707–1778) gave us our classification of species and genus; Captain James Cook set out to explore the Pacific on three separate voyages between 1768 and 1779; and in 1755 Dr. Sam-uel Johnson produced his *Dictionary of the English Language.*

Enlightenment thinkers sought to apply the same scientific methodology to economic, social, and politi-cal institutions and behavior. Adam Smith, in *Wealth of Nations* (1776), argued that government interfer-ence in economic affairs violated the interplay of natu-ral forces. (Try that argument on the IRS sometime.) Immanuel Kant (1724–1804) applied systematic rules to wars of the State. In France, applied methodology produced the *Encyclopédie,* a comprehensive, systematic collection of knowledge whose first volume (of twenty-eight) appeared in 1751. Edited by Denis Diderot and Jean d'Alembert, the *Encyclopédie* was also a forum for the premier representatives of enlightened thought, who wrote many of its articles and gave the work a distinctly liberal, progressive slant. This generated a great deal of controversy. The *Encyclopédie* was attacked by the Church and even banned by Louis XV at one point. It was similar to Madonna's book, *Sex.* Although everyone read it, no one would admit to owning a copy. Naturally, all this controversy turned out to be great publicity for both the *Encyclopédie* and its champi-

A diagram from the Encyclopédie *illustrates the components of an iron-shaping machine. The contraption was pretty good at cracking walnuts, too.*

ons of enlightened thought—the French *philosophes* Rousseau, Montesquieu, and Voltaire.

THE *PHILOSOPHES*

The *philosophes* of eighteenth-century France were neither revolutionaries nor necessarily reformers. Nevertheless, their attacks upon existing institutions, and their view that the human condition was improvable, provided a philosophical alternative to traditional—and increasingly irrelevant—thought. Self-confident, argumentative, and clever, the *philosophes* were more propagandists then academicians. They sought to spread their ideas as widely as possible, from the salons of Paris to the Russian capital, through pamphlets, letters, and gatherings of fellow thinkers.

They were hardly unanimous in their writings. Montesquieu was often criticized by his fellow thinkers for being too conservative. Jean-Jacques Rousseau's *Social Contract* (1762) elaborated the concept of "inalienable rights" and the blessings of popular government, but some of his peers derided him for being too radical. And like an enlightened Rush Limbaugh, Voltaire was often criticized simply for being too witty, too acerbic, or too popular.

What bound these men as *philosophes* was their condemnation of the *ancien régime* as a way of life. Both Voltaire and Montesquieu spent time in England, were energized by the individual liberty they found there, and often pointed across the channel to show the benefits of liberty and reason. They opposed both social distinctions based on birth and governmental policies

Quick-witted, entertaining, sarcastic, Voltaire had a seesaw relationship with Europe's rulers: one day a favorite of the court, the next day thrown into prison or told to leave the country.

developed by happenstance but maintained for tradition's sake. They argued that the individual had "natural rights" which government must never obstruct.
Therefore, any governing state must be properly *consti-
tuted,* and its powers explicitly spelled out in a
constitution.

The *philosophes,* for all their denunciation of the
present order, never dreamt that their ideas would
form the backbone of a revolution destroying that
order. If they anticipated anything from their trumpeting of natural rights and the failure of the *ancien*

"THE NATURAL RIGHTS OF MAN MUST NOT BE . . . EXCUSE ME, IS THAT CAVIAR?"

Great philosophical movements always have physical
hubs. The Greeks had the Academy, the French *philosophes* had . . . the salon. In an age of royal censorship, the *philosophes* spread their radical doctrines
by discussing them in salons, the eighteenth-century
equivalent of the celebrity cocktail party. Then, as
now, the hostess ruled, choosing guests on the basis
of their wittiness, sauciness, popularity, and ability
to create a stir without causing a scandal. Competition among *philosophes* for the favor of a reigning
hostess, as well as among the hostesses themselves, was fierce. It took real talent to speak about
something as serious as individual liberty in a super-
ficial, entertaining, amusing manner. Voltaire ex-
celled at it, even reveled in it. Rousseau—sensitive,
trusting, and honest—was completely out of place,
like Forrest Gump on *Meet the Press.*

régime, it was that the State might itself become enlightened—and so introduce reform. In fact, this is
what happened—outside France's borders.

Enlightened Despots

A handful of eighteenth-century rulers adopted enlightened policies and reforms. But their administrative, educational, and economic reforms were
motivated by self-interest, not by their belief in the
natural rights of the individual. They realized that a
prosperous, industrious populace was a better guaran-
tee of dynastic continuity than a grumbling mob of
malcontents. Four monarchs who made this brilliant
leap of faith were:

- Frederick II of Prussia (1712–1786),
  called Frederick the Great;
- Catherine II of Russia (1729–1796),
  called Catherine the Great;
- Maria Theresa of Austria (1717–1780)
  called Maria Theresa;
- Joseph II (1741–1790) of Austria,
  called Mr. Hapsburg, (by Thomas
  Jefferson, anyway).

Frederick entertained Voltaire at his court, until it
became clear that Prussia wasn't big enough for both
their egos, and maintained a regular correspondence
with the Frenchman after his departure. Under Frederick, Prussia became a haven of religious tolerance,

A quartet of "enlightened despots."
Frederick II of Prussia, (top left)
Catherine II of Russia, (top right)
Maria Theresa of Austria, (above, left)
and Joseph II of Austria. (above, right)

improved justice, and economic innovation—and, not incidentally, a European powerhouse. Diderot found favor with Catherine, as did Montesquieu, but her enlightenment was little more than lip service. Maria Theresa, Joseph II's mother, is remembered for the statement: "I do not belong to myself but only to the Republic."

Whatever his motives, Joseph II (1741–1790) was the most ambitious reformer of them all. One of Maria Theresa's sixteen children, in his ten years as emperor he issued a thousand decrees in all manner of reform—the so-called "Thousand Points of Enlightenment." He introduced the idea of numbering houses to expedite mail delivery, required that for every tree cut down in Vienna another had to be planted (a decree still in force), assured judicial and administrative reform, abolished serfdom, and issued the Patent of Toleration (1781), which allowed the public practice of the Protestant faith. At one point he even ordered that trap doors be placed on coffins, so that bodies could be ejected at the cemetery and the coffin reused. (This reform died quickly.) Joseph's fervor for reform outpaced that of his subjects, who eventually revolted in the face of such enlightened activity.

But in France, the ruling order's inability—or unwillingness—to respond to progressive development led not to revolt but to revolution.

You Say You Want
a Revolution?

When King Louis XVI returned from hunting on July 14, 1789, he was told by one of his noblemen that the Bastille had been stormed.

"Then it's a revolt," remarked the king.

"No, sire, it is a revolution," the nobleman replied.

He was right. What began that day was not another bread riot, but the cataclysmic end of Louis XVI's world order. For the next ten years, following the downfall of the *ancien régime,* governments would come and go—usually violently—with whirlwind speed. Political leaders rose from the mob, seized power, and declared permanent reforms that disappeared faster than *Wayne's World II.* Political shifts, alliances, betrayals, and beheadings occurred at a dizzying rate that can only be called modern, as leaders and ideas battled each other for their fifteen minutes of glory. And throughout this constant inconstancy, war. No series of events in Europe's history had been so dramatic in appearance, so charged with ideology, so violent in realization. A telling historical anecdote speaks of one famous Frenchman who, when asked what of consequence he had done during the French Revolution, replied: "I lived."

Revolutions, like earthquakes, are easy to predict once they've already occurred. The standard model for revolution (yes, there is one) explains that revolution, rather than revolt, occurs whenever the existing order is either incapable or unwilling to respond to the times. In social, political, and economic terms, France's *ancien*

"Why aren't these people working!"

régime was utterly incapable of responding to recent developments, because:

- A century of colonial and dynastic wars had left France at the edge of bankruptcy; bankrolling the American Revolution pushed her over the edge.
- The three estates no longer represented a stable distribution of wealth and political power. The bourgeoisie lacked representation in government that matched their crucial economic significance. The peasantry was being crushed under the burden of overtaxation. The nobility, having milked their estates dry and resisting fur-

ther taxation, wished to regain some of the power that they had lost under Louis XIV.

- The *philosophes* of the Enlightenment had provoked hope for the improvement of people's lot and provided the philosophical template for a new political order.
- The main representative of the *ancien régime*, Louis XVI, was an affable blunderer whose attempt to negotiate a path between reform and absolutism satisfied no one.

As in all political upheavals, it remained only for these currents to find a common place and time. In France's case the king himself brought them together.

"YOU MUST BE WONDERING WHY I CALLED YOU HERE"

In May of 1789 the king called the Estates-General to Versailles. This in itself was unusual, because no one had even seen the Estates-General since 1614, and almost no one remembered exactly how selecting the Estates-General was done. This body was an assembly of elected representatives from the three estates, convened by the king for advisory purposes. Each estate had its own political status and priority within the assembly, and each estate voted as a bloc, not as individuals. Although calling this gang together may seem like a fairly unwise move in retrospect, Louis had no other choice. With his country bankrupt, he needed to find new sources of income—even if it meant appealing to the disaffected.

Once seated, the Estates-General saw that a few things had changed since 1614. For one, half of the representatives were now from the Third Estate—600 out of the 1,200 in attendance. For another, a substantial number of representatives—most among the Third Estate, but a number of them liberals in the First and Second—wanted to change the voting rules to allow the Estates-General to vote as 1,200 individuals. Gridlock ensued, and the Estates-General broke up over the issue, with the majority refusing to participate until the voting rules were changed. Nobody went home, though. The reformers continued to meet, until one morning in June they were barred from their usual meeting place by the king, who insisted that they adhere to the old voting procedures.

Oops. The reformers occupied a local tennis court, where they redefined themselves as the National Constituent Assembly. The two qualifying adjectives tell the whole story: "National, to speak and act for the nation, not for one estate or only in the name of the king, and "Constituent," to give France a constitution.

The king once again attempted to play both sides against the middle, recognizing the National Assembly while at the same time calling royalist troops into the capital. This sparked popular riots that led to the storming of the Bastille, and within the year, Louis XVI was no longer king solely "by the grace of God" but "by the constitution" as well. His acknowledgment of this new fact of political life is painfully evident in

*"Let's lose the cap,
your Majesty.
While we're at it,
let's lose the head, too."*

the portrait where he poses with a revolutionary cap on his head.

Once the king had submitted to a constitution there was nothing to prevent the further dilution of his authority. The National Assembly, for all intents and purposes, now ruled France—and ruled it with fervor, dismantling the *ancien régime* bit by bit. Church property was seized, traditional privilege was abolished, and new administrative bodies were established.

NOW THAT'S WHAT I CALL "SPIN CONTROL"
. . . .
The storming of the Bastille was a failure as an event but tremendously significant as a phenomenon. The Bastille, a Paris fortress once used to house political prisoners, was stormed by revolutionaries who believed they would find ammunition stored there. They were wrong, so they freed the Bastille's prisoners— all seven of them. Sounds like a bust, right? Well, it wasn't long before news of this non-event spread, and the country learned that the unthinkable had occurred: a popular uprising against the despotic State. Thus a fizzled search for ammo became a symbol of the struggle against tyranny. That's why July 14th, Bastille Day, is the French national holiday (I'd call it their Fourth of July, but that would be chauvinistic.)

FAREWELL TO THE KING

Louis XVI, ever the ineffectual operator, aroused the revolutionaries' suspicion with intrigues against the constitution he had recently accepted. In 1791 when Louis and his queen, Marie Antoinette, attempted to flee to Hapsburg lands, they were captured and forcibly returned to Paris. The revolutionaries were further alarmed by the activities of foreign monarchs, who had massed an army to come to Louis's aid.

Hampered by royalist commanders who often assisted the invading Austrians, and ever suspicious of monarchist plots within France, the revolutionary government abolished the monarchy. On September 21, 1792, France became the first republic in a major European country. The king, now simply "Citizen Capet" (the family name of the first royals in France), was ignominiously placed in jail. On January 21, 1793, he was guillotined before a cheering crowd. Marie Antoinette followed ten months later, as did thousands more in the Reign of Terror that followed.

THE REIGN OF TERROR

The Reign of Terror (1793–1794) was a dreadful expression of revolutionary excess, provoked by fear and uncertainty. Amid the shambles of an old order and the instability of newly established institutions, France's leaders waged a terrible campaign against enemies of the Revolution, real and imagined, within and without France's borders.

For the next seven years, despite wide swings in character and membership, the revolutionary government would be at war with most of Europe. Because of the changing array of forces allied against France, wars during this period are known as Wars of the Coalitions, coalitions that have extended well beyond the end of the Revolution.

While war created havoc abroad, fanatic zeal created bloodshed at home. Fear of agitation by aristocratic émigrés abroad, and paranoia over possible counter-revolutionaries at home, fueled the Reign of Terror. These days the word "terror" pops up in every rotten movie. But when they say Reign of Terror they mean it. Chances were if you were popular with the in-crowd on Thursday, by Monday the same crowd would be cheering your trip to the guillotine. There were so many people to do away with—estimates hover around 11,000—that a kind of cottage industry in capital punishment sprang up. One patriotic citizen came up with

HERE'S YOUR CHAPEAU. WHAT'S YOUR HURRY?

Émigré is French for emigrant, but the word assumed a specific meaning during the French Revolution. Aristocrats and clergymen, who didn't particularly care for the revolutionaries' habit of confiscating heads, fled to friendly territories in Austria and England, where they fomented plots to restore the king. The revolutionaries officially declared them *émigrés*, which was really a death sentence in absentia. When Louis XVI was guillotined, the *émigrés* declared that Louis's son was now king, a move which can only have hastened the 10-year-old's own demise. The next person they declared king (in case you lost track, he was Louis XVIII) was the Comte de Provence (1755–1824), who knew enough to stay out of France. He didn't return until Napoleon's Waterloo, at which point everyone agreed he was, in fact, king.

The revolutionary intrigues of the *émigrés* inspired Hungarian writer Baroness Orczy to create England's Sir Percy Blakeney, whose foppish facade masked his secret efforts to rescue French nobles from the Revolution—as the Scarlet Pimpernel.

the idea of shackling a bunch of prisoners to a boat and then sinking it. This scientific approach to killing was, sadly enough, but an omen of things to come.

The particular agency responsible for this carnage was the Committee of Public Safety, a title about as appropriate as "MTV News." Its most infamous figure was Maximilien Robespierre, called "the Incorruptible." A more appropriate name would have been "le Terminator." Single-minded, ascetic, and inexhaustible, Robespierre personified the radical revolution—right up until July 25, 1794, when he, too, was guillotined. A famous cartoon of the time showed a snake biting its tail, with a caption that read: "The revolution devours its own."

Maximilien Robespierre: The head of the Committee of Public Safety was a dangerous man.

WHOSE SIDE ARE YOU ON, ANYWAY?

In an era of war and revolution, some guys had all the luck. Take Charles-Maurice de Talleyrand-Périgord (1754–1838), known simply as Talleyrand because his whole name wouldn't fit on the back of his softball jersey. Like a waiter walking through a food fight with a tray of dishes, Talleyrand managed to steer himself right into old age. Here's his *curriculum vitae:*

1780: Appointed agent-general of the clergy.

1791: Resigned clergy in support of National Assembly.

1792: In London as representative of French government.

1793: Listed as dangerous *émigré* by French government.

1794: Expelled from England as French national.

1796: Prime minister under the Directory.

1799: Assisted in coup d'etat against the Directory.

1800: Napoleon's foreign minister.

1814: Assisted restoration of Bourbons at Napoleon's expense.

1832: Ambassador to Great Britain.

1838: Dead (presumably of sheer exhaustion).

What do you call someone who could build a successful career by supporting just the right fanatics, paranoiacs, evangelical executioners, and revolutionary zealots? A diplomat.

Robespierre's death signaled a reactionary movement that ended the Reign of Terror. The Committee of Public Safety was eliminated, and the Directory (1795–1799) was formed—an oligarchic arrangement whereby a rotating directorship of five men, elected by the national legislature, held executive power. Naturally, such a government by committee was practically an invitation for a coup d'etat that would effectively end the Revolution.

The revolutionaries believed in the universality of

WHEN PLUVIÔSE SHOWERS COME YOUR WAY. . .

The revolutionaries' iconoclasm didn't end with simply beheading the king. No, they had to go and change the calendar as well. In 1793, to commemorate the birth of the French Republic, they created the Republican calendar. Following the systemic bent of the day, the revolutionaries divided the year into twelve months of thirty days, and gave the months names like Brumaire, Germinal, and Thermidor. Each month was divided into three *décades* of ten days. Of course, twelve times thirty comes to only 360, so the five days left over they turned into a long holiday at the end of their year (the middle of September). To top it off, they started numbering the years all over again. This must have been very confusing to people who had already planned birthday parties. In 1805, Napoleon decided France had enough, and in Thermi—sorry, *August*—got rid of the Republican calendar.

their cause, assuming that France was simply the birth-place of a liberation that would encompass the world. Certainly, the sudden transformation of a European power from absolute monarchy to radical republic threw the state system into a spin. Austria's Leopold II put together a military alliance with Prussia to invade France (a natural move, since Marie Antoinette was his sister). Russia's Catherine the Great, who had previously entertained enlightened views, found them much less entertaining after the Revolution. Great Britain went to war against France . . . again. Yet while the Revolution sent shocks throughout Europe, in the end, it ruthlessly and utterly destroyed France's existing order without replacing it. That monumental task was accomplished not by Committee, Directory, or National Assembly, but by one man.

NAPOLEON

In an age replete with firebrands and revolutionaries, patriots and champions, Napoleon Bonaparte (1769–1821)—military genius, shrewd politician, tireless administrator, and ambitious leader—towers above them all. No other person has so marked a continent. Born in Corsica, son of a middle-class attorney, he rose to become Emperor of the French Republic. In his grasp of the opportunities offered within France, he emerged as the first great modern leader, for his power was based not on noble birth or privilege, but on personal talent, great ambition, and superb managerial skills.

*Napoleon was born on the island
of Corsica and died on the isle
of St. Helena. In between
he conquered a continent.*

If it was enough accomplishment for one French-man to have simply survived the French Revolution, consider what Napoleon achieved. After receiving military training in France, he supported Robespierre yet managed to survive his fall, distinguished himself in various campaigns, and in 1796 became commander of the French army in Italy. His campaign there against Austria was marked by brilliance and audacity and made him a hero in France. In 1798 Napoleon led an invasion of Egypt. Despite initial victories, he was forced to return to France when the British navy, under Admiral Horatio Nelson (1758–1805), severed his supply lines by diverting the French fleet at Egypt's Bay of Aboukir.

What he found at home was opportunity that suited his ambitions. The Directory was ineffectual; government, inefficient; corruption, rampant. What happened next is all too familiar to us modern types. Using the army as a political base, on November 9, 1799, Napoleon engineered a coup d'etat, wrote a new constitution, and declared that France was now a "consulate."

Although we think of Napoleon primarily as a military leader, his greatest achievement was in administration. Imaginative, forceful, and shrewd, Napoleon saw in the shambles that was France the tools to rebuild the country. When he became First Consul (a title corresponding to "Head Guy") the first thing he did was declare that the Revolution was over. (If only Robespierre had thought of that!) Napoleon created ministries and agencies that consolidated and centralized power, and he made Paris the seat of that power.

The Bank of France was created in 1800 to regulate finance. The Napoleonic Code followed in 1804 to set standards for personal behavior and property. The University of France was founded to control public education. Combining elements of both the *ancien régime* and the Revolutionary zealots, Napoleon produced a synthesis nothing short of miraculous.

NAPOLEONIC WARS

One thing that made Napoleon so popular at first was that when he wasn't winning battles, he was signing peace treaties. In 1799 the French were exhausted, both spiritually and financially, by seven years of uninterrupted war. Napoleon, after first beating up on the Austrians again in Italy, made peace with them in 1801. A year later he made peace with the hated English. All this peace allowed him to concentrate on putting his domestic policies to work.

In 1804 he felt comfortable enough to renew his military ambitions. He crowned himself emperor (a title corresponding to "Head Guy—and We're Not Kidding") and went out conquering. By 1807 he had defeated superior Russian and Austrian forces at Austerlitz (a textbook case in military audacity and efficiency), fragmented the Hapsburg empire, and bothered just about everyone else worth bothering. (In 1806 Holy Roman Emperor Francis II, fearing that Napoleon would come after his title, formally dissolved the largely ceremonial position. Henceforth Francis's Hapsburg line would be emperors of Austria only.) His leadership and success made him a hero to his soldiers, and instilled a nationalistic spirit at home as the French army continued to add to the empire. Ironically, Napoleon's victories, by inspiring national-

THE CORSICAN BROTHERS

The four Bonaparte brothers (there were also three sisters) had a royal time in Europe, courtesy of over-achiever Napoleon.

Joseph (1768–1844) became king of Naples, later king of Spain.

Napoleon (1769–1821), emperor of France.

Louis (1778–1846) was king of Holland. His son,

Louis Napoleon (1808–1873), would later become Napoleon III.

Jerome (1784–1860) became king of Westphalia. His grandson by an American wife (Napoleon had the marriage annulled),

Charles Joseph Bonaparte (1851–1921), became Secretary of the Navy under Theodore Roosevelt.

And then there was brother Lucien (1775–1840), a true republican who opposed his brother's imperial rule. Ironically, *he* was the one the British captured, while on a ship bound for America.

ist fervor in French-occupied territories, also helped lay the foundation for his defeat. His habit of replacing local rulers with relatives and military comrades helped to unite conquered populations against France, who naturally tended to cast their struggle against the French nation in nationalistic terms.

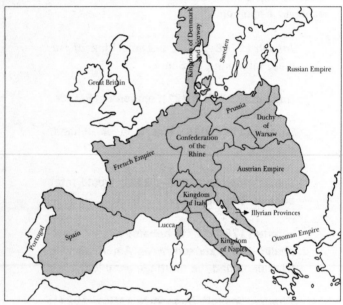

Napoleonic empire at its height (1812).

Napoleon's downfall, like everything else about him, was epic. He invaded Russia with 300,000 men in June 1812. Seeking a quick, decisive blow to the Russian forces, he moved swiftly to engage them. But the Russian armies, rather than fight, retreated as quickly as the French pursued. They knew what they were doing.

The French army hurried into the heart of the immense country, stretching their supply lines to the breaking point. When they looked to the countryside to support them, they found that the Russians had burned everything in sight. Napoleon reached Moscow with half of his army after a terrible battle at Borodino, only to find the city empty and ablaze. When peace overtures to the czar fell on deaf ears, Napoleon began his retreat. Winter was coming.

Most of the French army never left Russia. Many died as Russian forces attacked the long column of retreating soldiers almost at will. Many starved. And thousands simply dropped in their tracks to freeze in the brutal Russian winter. Of the 300,000 who had entered Russia, less than 70,000 made it back out—only to be set upon by an alliance of Russian, Austrian, and Prussian forces. By the time he left Russia, Napoleon's army had been crushed by the immensity of a country as large as his ambition.

EXILE AND WATERLOO

As he had cast his shadow over the map of Europe, so now Napoleon was dwarfed by the alliance of powers against him, notably Russia, Great Britain, Prussia, and Austria. After defeat at the Battle of Leipzig (1813), he abdicated in 1814 in the face of an invading army. Louis XVI's brother was invited to rule as a constitutional monarch, Napoleon's empire was dismantled, and Napoleon himself was exiled to the island of Elba.

He didn't stay there long. Having beaten the

French, the powers of the alliance were now squabbling among themselves. Hearing of this, seizing upon popular dissatisfaction with the restored monarchy, recognizing France's displeasure at being a vanquished nation, Napoleon left Elba in 1815. Assembling an army, he marched to Paris and announced the restoration of the empire.

Naturally, this simply gave the squabblers something to agree on again. Napoleon's army was met at Waterloo (in present-day Belgium) by the combined forces of England and Prussia, and the emperor was again defeated. Abdication and exile to the island of St. Helena followed, and this time there was no return. The second incarnation of Napoleon's empire had lasted just one hundred days. Yet such is the measure of the man that this period is called "the Hundred Days," and the site of his final defeat has become a permanent part of our language.

SUMMARY

The Enlightenment, the most influential intellectual movement of the modern era, emphasized the power of reason, the benefits of liberty, and the idea that ability, not birth, should decide one's place in the world.

Dynastic wars, conducted within the framework of the new European state system, marked most of the century, financially weakening France.

France's *ancien régime* was unable to accommodate the economic rise and political consciousness of the middle class, the liberal propaganda of the *philosophes,* and the financial strains of a century of war. Its rigidity turned to rigor mortis as the French Revolution introduced the idea of representative government in European political thought and practice.

The eighteenth century ended and the nineteenth began with the Napoleonic Era, named after the single individual whose empire-building upset the balance of power of an entire continent and established the structure of the modern state: a centralized system of government administering through uniform codes and standards.

Rather than seek to dominate Europe, each of the great powers—Great Britain, France, Russia, Austria, and Prussia—sought to maintain a "balance of power" between them.

CHAPTER 2

POLITICAL REACTION AND INDUSTRIAL DEVELOPMENT
(1815–1870)

YOU MUST REMEMBER THIS

Absolutism tried to make a comeback in the nineteenth century, but only managed to postpone—not defeat—the liberal aspirations of an increasingly urban population.

IMPORTANT EVENTS

★ Congress of Vienna, 1814–1815
★ Defeat of Napoleon at Waterloo, 1815
★ Opening of the first steam railroad line between Darlington and Stockton in England, 1825
★ July Revolution in France, 1830
★ Publication of *The Communist Manifesto,* 1848
★ Revolutions throughout Europe, 1848
★ Crimean War between Russia and Great Britain, France, and Turkey, 1853–1856
★ Opening of the Suez Canal, 1869
★ Unification of Germany and Italy, 1871

Napoleon so dominated Europe that his defeat left the Continent groping for an identity. At the Congress of Vienna, an 1815 gathering of European powers led by the Austrian chancellor, Metternich, conservatives sought to throw a new coat of paint over the same old absolutist forms of government and forget the last quarter century. The middle class, however, wanted representational government responsible to its citizens, not its rulers. As a result, the nineteenth century saw a constant struggle between reaction and revolution.

In the end, absolutist rule was defeated not so much by revolution as by irrelevance. If the *ancien régime* had been inappropriate in 1789, it could only be more so after 1815. The liberal bourgeoisie no longer had their French Revolution, but the Industrial Revolution would serve them better. Bankers and entrepreneurs—not kings and bishops—grew to predominance, stripping absolutist regimes of any pretense to economic legitimacy. The name of the game was no longer chess, but Monopoly, as steam engines powered Europe into the modern age.

YESTERDAY ONCE MORE

Following Napoleon's defeat and exile to Elba, the victorious powers—Great Britain, Russia, Austria, and Prussia—had to figure out what to do with the shambles of his empire. Seizing upon the opportunity not just to reconstruct Europe but also to eat and drink to excess, the major powers got together at the Congress of Vienna (1814). Everybody who was anybody

WHO'S
H
O
☞

Movers and Shakers

Otto von Bismarck (1815–1898): Chancellor of Prussia and then of Germany, the architect of German unity.

Charles Dickens (1812–1870): The best of novelists and the worst of novelists.

Karl Marx (1818–1883): Philosopher and social critic who developed the concept of "class warfare" and denounced modern capitalism.

Napoleon III (1808–1873): Nephew of Napoleon I, president of France (1848–1852), then emperor of France (1852–1871), then prisoner of Prussia (1870), finally exile in England.

Queen Victoria (1819–1901): Queen of England (1837–1901), whose reign has been called the "Victorian Age."

Prince Klemens Wenzel Nepomuk Lothar von Metternich (1773–1859): Chancellor of Austria, designer of the Quadruple Alliance, and yet one more guy whose name is longer than his lifetime.

Charles Darwin (1809–1882): English naturalist whose *On the Origin of Species* (1859) proved an evolutionary work.

was there. Rulers, ministers, and diplomats from all the major states attended, with Austria's chancellor, Prince Klemens von Metternich (1773–1859), serving as host. Everyone was having such a good time that no one noticed when, in 1815, Napoleon sneaked back to Paris, assembled an army, and declared himself emperor again. British general Arthur Wellesley (1769–1852), whose success against Napoleon's armies had earned him the title Duke of Wellington, was in Vienna as Great Britain's representative. Hearing of Napoleon's return, Wellesley excused himself, grabbed a few English and Prussian troops, and routed Napoleon at Waterloo once and for all. He made it back to Vienna in time for dessert.

The Congress was a huge success—socially, that is. It gave Vienna its reputation as the city of wine, women, and song. An Austrian diplomat remarked: "The Congress does not work; it dances." Politics was never allowed to interfere with partying. In fact, the Congress never actually met as a formal body. Its decisions were made informally by the four major players.

Like all other parties, the host here determined the theme. In Vienna it turned out to be "Everything Old Is New Again." Metternich, an intelligent and dogged conservative, loathed the liberal ideals of the French Revolution. Believing the *ancien régime* to have been the pinnacle of European civilization, he and other like-minded participants (notably Czar Alexander I) fought for the restoration of the old order. They succeeded. In the end, Europe as reconstructed by the Congress was a genuinely reproduced antique, highlighted by the restoration of most of the old monarchies.

The Congress returned Lombardy (which Napoleon had seized) to Austria—and threw in Venice for good measure. Belgium and the Netherlands were joined to become the Kingdom of Holland, a move that satisfied everyone except the residents of Belgium and the Netherlands. The Confederation of Germany was established, in which thirty-nine states were loosely bound under Austria. France, the Big Loser, wasn't even invited, but crashed the party anyway in the form of that skillful opportunist, Talleyrand, whom we encountered in the previous chapter. He managed to secure a role in the proceedings for the restored Bourbon monarchy under Louis XVIII.

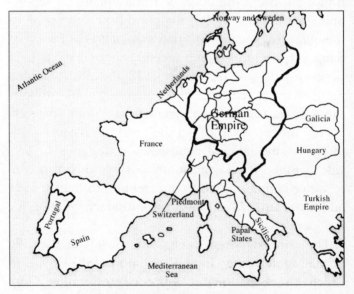

Absolutism: The Sequel, or Europe
after the Congress of Vienna, 1815.

The Congress handed out party favors to the celebrants as well. Prussia received territory along the Rhine and got half of Poland; the other half became a Russian-dominated Kingdom of Poland. Great Britain got dibs on Capetown in South Africa, as well as the island of Malta. The opportunity to grab whole chunks of real estate made this a festive time, indeed.

THE CONCERT SYSTEM

In order to safeguard their re-creation of Europe, the four victorious powers proved they could count by forming the Quadruple Alliance. Intended to prevent future disorder, whether it be revolutionary or Napoleonic, the alliance called for periodic meetings of its members to decide international matters. To everyone's surprise, three such meetings were actually held between 1815 and 1823. After 1818, the alliance added France as a participating member, but nobody thought to call the arrangement a "quintuple alliance." Instead it was called the "concert system." This effort at international collusion was designed to provide a united front against any possible threat to conservative regimes. It led to intervention in Italy in 1821 and Spain in 1823 to quash revolutionary agitation for independence.

The concert system even came down on the side of liberation in the Greek Revolution (1821–1830), in which Greek nationalists opposed continuing Ottoman (Turkish) domination. Russia jumped in to support the Greek bid for independence, hoping to extend her influence in the region. England and France got on board to dilute unilateral Russian support of the Greeks. It was the concert system at its best, with everyone operating out of either greed or fear.

Metternich's work succeeded in reestablishing the balance of power in Europe. As a result, international relations during the first half of the nineteenth century were remarkably smooth. War, when it did occur, was smaller and shorter than in the preceding and following centuries. (Not to worry, though. Progress, in the form of mining disasters, industrial accidents, and disease, took up the slack in killing.) But the conservative political foundation of post-Napoleonic Europe was at odds with liberal popular sentiment. Europe, as reconstructed by the Congress of Vienna and supported by the Quadruple Alliance, turned out to be the Eurodisney of its day: out of place, out of date, and roundly attacked from within.

As much as Metternich and his pals wanted to pretend otherwise, it was impossible to stuff the revolutionary genie back into its bottle. Absolutism was on its way out; liberalism, on its way in. Liberal was nineteenth-century shorthand for "bourgeois, capitalist, individualist, no-taxation-without-representation reformer." The ideas of the Enlightenment—the emphasis on reason, individual liberty and potential, its passion for scientific research and progress—had been adopted as a creed by the educated middle class. Having endured years of revolution and war, they were ill-disposed to accept Metternich's vision of yesterday and agitated for political reforms that would reflect their economic and social significance: constitutionalism and the right to vote. Their demand for proper representation was only strengthened by the progress of industrialization. Increasingly, economic prosperity centered not around farms or palaces but around cities—where the factories, shipyards, and railroads were in the hands of the middle class.

THE YOUNG AND THE RESTLESS

The resurrected old order discovered it had to deal with a couple of new political players: an increasingly urban labor force and a burgeoning student population—each owing its emergence to the rise of the bourgeoisie. The gradual shift to an urban, industrial economy drew increasing numbers of laborers into the cities. Living side by side in smoke-choked "developments," they suffered the consequences of breakneck progress: overcrowding, crime, disease, cruel working hours and conditions. But living side by side also enabled them to organize into trade unions, fraternal societies, and political organizations. For the first time, labor became a factor in politics. Oppressed politically by conservatives, economically by liberals, and socially by just about everyone, labor was almost always willing to join in a protest, riot, or revolution.

Idealism and youth drove the student population into the fray. Revolutionary faith in science and reason had produced a boom in education, as scientific research—not religious dogma—became the academic motto. Although far inferior in numbers than their bourgeois or proletarian allies, students supplied the passion and idealism so necessary to meaningful political change. More and more students, inspired by academic freedom and emboldened by youth, sought to bring freedom to the political arena—often returning empty-handed to class with the excuse: "The revolution ate my homework."

SPRING FORWARD, FALL BACK

Sooner or later, conservatism was bound to be swamped by the formidable array of *-isms* aligned against it: liberalism, individualism, industrialism, capitalism, and eventually, nationalism. While most liberals were reformist in disposition, seeking change through parliamentary procedures, others saw revolution as the only effective means of positive change. Even Thomas Jefferson entertained such thoughts. "I hold it that a little rebellion, now and then, is a good thing, and as necessary in the political world as storms in the physical," he wrote to James Madison on January 30, 1787. When economic conditions spurred laborers to add their voices to that of the middle class, a little rebellion is what most countries got. Riots and revolts continued to pop up sporadically until 1830, when France set off a wave of European revolution.

Since succeeding Louis XVIII in 1824, King Charles X had been pushing the absolutist envelope—flaunting his preference for the clergy and aristocracy, appointing ministers whose policies denied the events of the last century, making reparations to dispossessed *émigrés*. In 1830, when national elections returned a legis-

lature overwhelmingly opposed to his absolutist
revisionism, Charles muzzled the press, outlawed public assembly, and declared the elections void. This only
ensured that he would be the last of the Bourbon
rulers. Liberal factions quickly took to the barricades,
and after three days of fighting, Paris was in the hands
of revolutionaries. Charles, obviously up on his family
history, realized what happens to monarchs who stick
around when they're not wanted and fled the country.
Fearing that the establishment of another republic
would simply provoke Metternich and his monarchist
buddies to stomp on France again, the liberals opted
simply to elect a new, improved king—not a member
of Charles's Bourbon house, but a cousin from the
Orleans line, Louis Philippe.

Revolutionary tactic or performance art?

BEFORE GARAGE SALES: REVOLUTIONARY BARRICADES

A revolutionary folk art was the erection of barricades. These obstacles, which divided those folk rising up from those trying to put them down, were crude defense works piled up across streets. The narrowness of the city streets and the relative ineffectiveness of muskets and rifle fire (rolling cannon in wasn't easy, again because of the width and twist of the streets) made barricades both easy and effective. Anything available was tossed into the pile. Cobblestones pulled up from the street were handiest (most cobblestones were, as they still are in much of Europe, laid in a bed of sand), but old bedding, wagons, chopped down trees, and barrels were thrown in for good measure. Among recent manifestations of this folk practice, the Student Revolts of 1968 in Paris produced a new element: the extensive use of overturned cars.

France's revolution set off similar uprisings in Poland, Italy, Germany, and Switzerland, which were duly put down by their ruling governments. Outside France, only in the Netherlands did revolution succeed, as Belgium became a constitutional monarchy in her own right (1831). But revolution denied turned out to be revolution delayed, for within two decades conditions would spark another round of it. Only Russia and Great Britain, one at each end of the revolutionary scale, were immune to the uprisings that plagued Europe.

"So, how does it feel to be taking part in history?"

PARLIAMENT ACTS;
RUSSIA REACTS

Great Britain continued to make use of her head start over the Continent in political change. Economic hardship and political dissent in England resulted in riot and reform, not revolution. The Reform Act of 1832 redistributed seats in Parliament and reduced property restrictions on eligibility for office—a move that greatly benefited the cash-heavy, land-light middle class. The Chartist movement (1836–1848), a coalition of workers, political agitators, and reformers, wasn't satisfied by the Reform Act. The Chartists wanted universal manhood suffrage, a secret ballot, and salaries for members of Parliament (so that men other than the well-off could run). The Chartists presented to Parliament the Great Charter of 1839, a large roll containing some 2 million names, as a petition of grievances and a demand for further reform. Moving with its customary lightning speed, the government reacted eighteen years later with a second Reform Act, doubling the electorate to over 2 million by reducing voting qualifications. The wishes of the Chartists were largely fulfilled in 1884 by a last Reform Act which instituted universal manhood suffrage. Pity that the Chartist movement itself had died out some years back.

If England was at the head of the liberal-industrial conga line, Russia brought up the tail. Czar Nicholas I succeeded his brother Alexander in 1825 only by putting down a revolt by army reformers. For the rest of his rule he dealt severely with any sign of liberal agitation. The Polish Revolution of 1831, inspired by the French one of 1830, aimed at the expulsion of Russian troops from the country and the establishment of a republic. It achieved the opposite. When Nicholas responded with military force, the Polish revolutionaries fled and Russian control was reestablished even more stringently. The Polish Revolution of 1863–1864 met a similar fate, despite the protests of England, Austria, and France. Inside Russia, Nicholas clamped down on academic freedom, increased censorship, and built up the czarist secret police.

The one reform of significance in Russia was the abolition of serfdom through the Emancipation Edict of 1861—a measure taken by Nicholas's successor, Alexander II, as an economic necessity due to Russian losses in the Crimean War (1853–1856). Russia responded to the call for liberal reform haltingly, grudgingly, and only when absolutely necessary—a policy that insulated them from the outbreaks of 1848.

THE REVOLUTIONS OF 1848

The spring of 1848 witnessed major revolutions in France, Germany, Austria, Hungary, and Italy. As with previous versions, political demand and economic need sparked the uprisings. The European liberals' continuing call for extension of the electorate and responsible government coincided with a continent-wide depression and a food shortage caused by the Potato Famine, resulting from a blight that ruined the crop. It was felt most severely in Ireland, where *2 million* people either emigrated (mostly to America) or starved, causing a 25 percent drop in that country's population.

There was also a significant new twist to these revolutions, one that had been building for some time now: nationalism. The eighteenth century had seen the erosion of institutions with which people had once identified themselves. Prior to the French Revolution, if someone asked who you were, you'd probably claim membership in one of three groups: the church, your feudal lord, or whatever ruling dynasty was in power. (There was, as yet, no Jerry Lewis Fan Club.) But in 1789, the creation of France's National Assembly provided an alternative: neither worshiper, serf, nor subject, but citizen. Napoleon also fostered the idea with his uniform civil code and expansion of the educational system, enhancing linguistic and legal ties between Frenchmen of all strata.

Nationalism was also popularized by Giuseppe Mazzini (1805–1872), founder of an organization called Young Italy, whose goal was the political unification of that peninsula. The surest path to prosperity, he reasoned, was the creation of a nation-state, wherein a single nationality could be supported by a single, responsible government. Although he was liberal in disposition, his ideas had an ethnic ring: He believed that each people had distinctive qualities. Nineteenth-century nationalists rarely considered the flip side of ethnic nationalism, one all too common in our times: chauvinistic intolerance and ethnic cleansing. Mazzini's own idealism is best expressed by his view that harmony in Europe, like that in a choral concert, would be achieved if each people sang its parts.

What the people were singing in 1848 was "Wild in the Streets." Disparate groups were united in the denunciation of government. The middle class loosened its collar and shook hands with the working class; university students joined them in the streets, shouting slogans, waving arms, avoiding class. These young folk even added a certain sartorial dash: the University of Vienna's "Academic Legion" had colorful uniforms with scarlet-lined cloaks. (Weapons might have been a better idea.)

Once again, the trouble began in France, where Louis Philippe's response to the demand for an enlargement of the franchise was the imperative of his prime minister, François Guizot: *Enrichissez-vous!* ("get rich"). The popular response to his suggestion is unprintable. The king, after consulting the "Berlitz Handbook to Getting Overthrown," restricted public assembly. Liberals responded with banquets, an exquisite French combination of ingestion and protestation, at which revolutionary speeches would be given over dessert. When this rubber-poulet circuit grew too popular, the government forbade a banquet to be held in Paris. The citizens, inspired and agitated by the cries and actions of university students, took to the streets, Louis Philippe took a hike, and this time there was no question of inviting another king to mess things up. The Second Republic was established.

In Austria, the old and senile Hapsburg Emperor Ferdinand was faced with uprisings by Czechs, Hun-

Louis Philippe, France's "bourgeois king."

garians, and Germans. He fled with his family to Inns-
bruck, where he soon abdicated in favor of his
eighteen-year-old nephew, Franz-Josef. Metternich himself resigned as chancellor and left Vienna. In the German states, liberals were invited to draft a constitution.
Across Europe, the old regime started handing out
constitutions to a demanding populace.

WINNING BY LOSING

In the short run, the revolutions of 1848 failed. Despite early liberal success, by 1849 many of the old
regimes had reestablished themselves. In Germany,
the effort to unite all German states under one constitution fell apart when Austria and Prussia couldn't get
along—neither would allow the other to dominate
such a union. The Italian Republic proclaimed by
Mazzini disintegrated in 1850 as Austrian troops re-
claimed territory from the revolutionaries. Combined
Austrian and Russian forces relieved Hungary of its
independence in 1849, six months after independence
had been won.

Many of these regimes paid lip service to reform by
retaining new assemblies and constitutions, but they
were far from democracies under republic rule.
Among the major powers, only France had a republic
in 1848, but its president was a man called Louis Napoleon Bonaparte. The nephew of Napoleon Bonaparte, he lived up to his name in 1851 by seizing
absolute control in a coup d'etat. The following year,
by means of a plebiscite, he became Napoleon III.

"FLED" SOUNDS SO MUCH BETTER
THAN "RAN AWAY"

Nineteenth-century Europe was a revolving door for nationalists, royalists, and provocateurs. Here's just a partial list of the notables who took forced vacations in England:

Giuseppe Mazzini: The Italian nationalist fled to England in 1837;

Karl Marx: Winner of the Revolutionary Pest Award, by 1848 he had been expelled from Belgium, Germany, and France;

Charles X: The absolutist Bourbon settled for scotch in 1830;

Louis Philippe: From citizen to exile king in one easy flight (1848);

Victor Hugo: Left France when the Second Republic was dissolved by Napoleon III. He lived on the isle of Guernsey from 1851 to 1866, where he wrote *Les Misérables* (1862).

The Creative Exile Award goes to Italy's revolutionary guerilla leader *Giuseppe Garibaldi.* Defeated by the Austrians in 1848, he spent five years on exotic Staten Island.

(Napoleon Bonaparte's son and designated successor, who died at 21, never got to reign. As a consolation prize he was given a number anyway, as well as a T-shirt that read, "My father went to Waterloo and all I got was this lousy roman numeral.")

In the long run, however, most of the objectives of the revolutionaries were realized. It was clear that absolutism was fighting a rearguard action. In 1853, in fact, the conservatives' cooperative effort at containing liberalism—the concert system—ended as war broke out in the Crimea.

THE CRIMEAN WAR

Control of the Black Sea and the Balkan territory around it had always been a sore point among the European powers. The region's strategic importance and commercial value attracted just about anyone with an army. Russia, in control of the northern shore (including the peninsula of the Crimea), was always trying to push its way south into Turkish territory—either politically or militarily. Everyone else worked to keep the Russians out. In 1823 Great Britain and France had joined Russia in assisting the Greek independence movement, simply to prevent Russia from becoming too influential in the region.

Angling for another way into the Balkans, Russia went to war against Turkey in 1829, and in 1833 ended up as protectorate of the entire Ottoman Empire. This solo act didn't sit too well with the other members of the concert system, who knew that for the Russians "protectorate" was just another way of saying "property." In 1841 the dissatisfied powers, led by France and Great Britain, managed to transform the Russian protectorate into a European protectorate. In this case, "protectorate" was just another way of saying, "Hold on while we get out our guns."

Czar Nicholas I grew tired of the French and English showing up and yelling, "Me, too!" every time he made some headway. In July 1853 he seized two Turkish territories under the pretext of protecting Christian residents of the Muslim Ottoman Empire. Turkey declared war. France and Great Britain, realizing that Turkey would lose without help, weighed in against Russia early the next year and were joined by Sardinia in 1855. Russia was quickly driven out of Turkish territory, but the allied forces against Russia were determined to win a decisive victory. In August 1855 they landed on the Crimean peninsula and launched a massive attack on the Russian stronghold at Sevastopol.

For the next year and a half, the participants in the Crimean War did their best to make it the worst war ever fought. The amount of useless carnage can best be judged from the fact that its most celebrated figures have little to do with military glory. Florence Nightingale (1820–1910) volunteered to command the British nursing services during the war—and became a legend. Photographer Roger Fenton (1819–1869), as the official war correspondent of the British government, exposed the brutality of the war to those back in England. And the officer who led the most famous, most celebrated action of the war, James

Cardigan (1797–1868) . . . well . . . had a sweater named after him. It should have been a bandage.

The war ended Russia's bid for control of the Balkans—for the time being, at least. Czar Nicholas had died in 1855. His son and successor, Alexander II, turned to domestic affairs, instigating internal reforms that would restore Russian might. More importantly, the war put an end to the last vestige of Metternich's resuscitated old order. The absence of an international coalition dedicated to preserving the status quo helped clear the way for the creation of two new nations: Italy and Germany.

JOIN THE OTTO CLUB

Both Camillo Cavour (1810–1861) of Sardinia and Prussia's Otto von Bismarck realized that nothing promotes unity quite like a common enemy. Bismarck made the point in his "Iron and Blood" speech of 1857, in which he remarked that nations are made not by parliamentary majorities but by "iron and blood." These two drove loose confederations of states to national unification through a common pattern: provocation of war, galvanization of public opinion, annexation of territory, and the assurance that one state within the new nation would dominate: Prussia in Germany, Sardinia in Italy.

Ever since the disintegration of the Holy Roman Empire, the German-speaking people had been divided into camps: Prussia and the Austrian Empire of the Hapsburgs. Naturally, the question of unification

*Otto von Bismarck,
the architect of
German unification.*

came up often. Both Austria and Prussia agreed that
unification was a wonderful idea. They just couldn't
agree who was going to be top dachshund. Within the
Germanic Confederation, Austria and Prussia maneu-
vered constantly for political and economic advantage.
Prussia made headway in 1831 by establishing a *Zoll-
verein* (customs union), which bound German states
together under Prussian leadership for the purpose of
easing trade.

Otto von Bismarck was determined to settle the unification question in Prussia's favor. In 1866, as minister to King William I, he took advantage of a minor
dispute over the provinces of Schleswig and Holstein
to launch the Seven Weeks' War against Austria. Prussia's swift victory voided the Germanic Confederation,
won control of the northern German states, and
earned Prussia a nasty reputation.

Next Bismarck turned his attention to the remaining German states. In order to bring them into the unification fold, Bismarck looked for a new common enemy and found an old one—France. It would be best, he knew, for France to declare war on Prussia, rather than the other way around. The Free German states would rally to his side much more readily if Prussia was the defender. How he managed this trick illustrates his deft diplomatic hand.

Bismarck engineered one of those wonderful succession controversies by offering a Prussian prince as candidate for the Spanish throne. Napoleon III didn't much care for being surrounded by Prussians (who would?) and demanded that the candidacy be withdrawn. The French foreign minister showed up at Ems, a German spa where the Prussian king, William I, was relaxing, with a message from Napoleon: withdraw the candidacy, apologize for making everyone upset about this, and promise never to do it again. This only steamed the king, who refused categorically. Bismarck got hold of the communiqué, did a little editing, and published the French demands. His slanted version of the message, known as the Ems Dispatch, heightened both French hostility and German chauvinism. In July 1870 Napoleon declared war on Prussia.

The French were no match for Prussia's military might and skill, and within two months Napoleon himself was forced to surrender on the battlefield at Sedan. Left with neither emperor nor king, the French played "Pin the Government on the Country"

CAN WE GET THIS RIGHT SOMEDAY?

Here's a fun recap of French rule from the French Revolution to the end of the Franco-Prussian War (1870–1871). Fasten your seat belts!

First Republic (1792–1797)—Robespierre and his pals

Consulate (1797–1804)—Consul Napoleon Bonaparte

Empire (1804–1814)—make that *Emperor* Napoleon I

Bourbon Monarchy (1814–1830) under Louis XVIII and Charles X—They're ba-a-ack

Orleans Monarchy (1830–1848)—under Louis Philippe

Second Republic (1848–1852)—President Louis Napoleon Bonaparte

Empire (1852–1870)—make that *Emperor* Napoleon III

Third Republic (est. 1870)

It's no wonder France is considered the birthplace of the shrug.

again, and came up with another republic. The southern German states knew a winner when they saw one and joined Prussia. With the crowning of William I in 1871, Bismarck had created a unified German Empire.

Like his renowned uncle, Napoleon III became emperor of France, saw his empire ruined by military defeat, and died in exile.

ITALIAN SUBVERSION

Similarly, the Sardinian prime minister, Camillo Cavour, built his own state into a solid base for unification. Most of Italy had been restored to Austria at the Congress of Vienna. Since then, however, a nationalist movement known as the *Risorgimento* (resurgence) had stirred up opposition to foreign domination. Although revolutionary movements were put down in 1830 and 1848, the defeats did produce national leaders—Camillo Cavour, Giuseppe Mazzini, and Giuseppe Garibaldi—as well as a geographic center for the movement—the Kingdom of Sardinia.

Cavour advanced Sardinia's claim to power by joining Great Britain and France in the Crimean War. Playing—and winning—with the big boys enhanced Sardinia's international reputation, and generated French and British goodwill. In 1858 Cavour entered into an alliance with France against Austria. In theensuing war, Sardinia won control of most of southern Italy. Even after Emperor Napoleon III backed out of the alliance, the drive for unification maintained

HOLY GRUDGE!
. . . .
Italian unification wasn't terribly popular with Pope Pius IX (1792–1878). As pope, he was also civil ruler of the Papal States, a sizable chunk of territory the papacy had governed since the eighth century. (In 1797 Napoleon I had taken it, of course, but the Congress of Vienna had given it back in 1815.) In 1871 not only were the Papal States forced to become part of the new Italy, but also Rome—site of the Vatican, the pope's headquarters—was made the capital. To protest the papacy's loss of independence and sovereignty, Pius IX went into the Vatican and never came out.

For the next fifty-eight years, every one of Pius IX's successors would follow his example, refusing to set

HOLY GRUDGE! (*continued*)
. . . .
foot outside the Vatican—until, in 1929, Benito Mussolini signed the Lateran Treaty, which created the independent state of Vatican City.

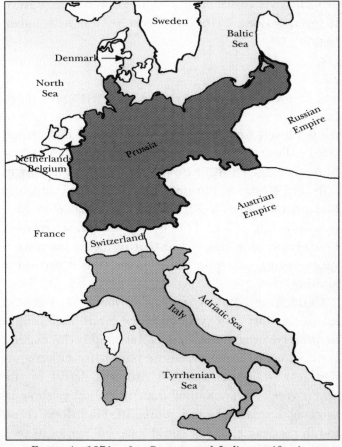

Europe in 1871, after German and Italian unification.

momentum as Sardinia gathered rebellious provinces to its tricolor banner. In 1860 Garibaldi liberated the kingdom of Sicily. The following year, the kingdom of Italy was declared and the king of Sardinia became its ruler. At that point only Venice and Rome were lacking. Italy was finally able to include them with the assistance of another unifying country—Prussia, whose victories over Austria in 1866 and France in 1870 freed these two cities to become part of the new Italian nation.

AUSTRIA ADDS A HYPHEN

After a lovely first half century, the second half proved simply disastrous for the Austrian empire. The Hapsburgs managed to put down the 1848 revolutions in Italy and Hungary, but only after the liberal uprisings had driven Emperor Ferdinand and Chancellor Metternich from office. The new emperor, 18-year-old Franz-Josef, soon discovered that restoring his conservative regime was one thing; preserving it was quite another.

German and Italian unification had cost Austria a lot of territory and prestige. Now Franz-Josef sought to preserve what remained of his empire by making concessions to Hungary, whose nationalist movements had revived in the wake of Austria's defeat in the Seven Weeks' War. Rather than risk another show of force against Hungarian nationalists, Franz-Josef chose to offer a deal: Hungary could have full run of its own domestic affairs, if it agreed to accept Franz-Josef as its ruler. The Hungarian leaders were no fools. They realized that, sitting between Russia and Austria as they were, they were going to have to be buddies with one of the two. They chose Schubert over Mussorgsky. In 1867 Franz-Josef became king of Hungary and the "dual monarchy" of Austria-Hungary was born.

MEDIC!

In 1859 at the Battle of Solferino, the Swiss Jean Henri Dunant witnessed the tremendous suffering wounded soldiers endured. He organized an all-volunteer effort for aiding soldiers wounded in battle, called the Red Cross. (Its symbol, a red cross on a white field—save in Turkey, where a red crescent is used—is easily spotted from a distance.) To make sure the organization could go about its humanitarian business without getting fired upon, in 1864 Dunant prompted the first Geneva Convention (in this sense an agreement, not a gathering). A dozen countries signed the pact, whereby it was declared inhumane to fire at someone giving aid to the guy you just tried to kill a few minutes ago.

For his efforts, in 1901 Dunant was awarded the first Nobel Peace Prize, endowed by the man whose nitroglycerin plant had blown up the same year the Red Cross was established.

THE INDUSTRIAL REVOLUTION

While unrest and revolution were transforming Europe's political landscape, a revolution of a different sort was transforming not just the landscape but also the world. The Industrial Revolution actually began in mid-eighteenth-century England with John Kay's flying shuttle (1733), James Hargreaves's spinning jenny (1760), Richard Arkwright's spinning frame (1869), and Samuel Crompton's spinning mule (1779)—not a bunch of circus acts, but a series of practical innovations in the textile industry. These machines made the process of yarn spinning speedy, cheap, and automatic. It's not hard to guess the effect on the textile industry of devices that saved labor, time, and money. Pretty soon every manufacturer wanted to be the first on his block to own one.

Once textile production became mechanized, a whole series of changes kicked in—changes that would eventually spread to other industries as they, too, put new technology to work for them. Efficiency dictated, naturally, that machines, materials, and labor should all be concentrated in one area. After all, it just wasn't done to ask some poor spinner to take a flying jenny home with him. As a result, large factories and mills were constructed, at first alongside rivers, whose waters powered the new machines; later—as steam engines replaced rivers in the late eighteenth century—in more convenient places, such as ports or major crossroads.

Great Britain led the way not simply because of technological innovation, but because it was uniquely prepared to take advantage of the new machines. Advances in production required new markets for the surplus of goods, and the colonizing British—with their long-standing partnership between government and business—had plenty of those, shipping cotton goods not just to the rest of Europe but also to Latin America, Africa, and the Orient. It didn't hurt, either, that Great Britain didn't have to worry about Napoleon's armies tramping all over the flower beds, as the rest of Europe did. Politically stable, domestically undisturbed, and economically sound, Great Britain made the most of mechanized production. By the middle of the nineteenth century, England had earned the title "workshop of the world."

That workshop was a factory. The system that developed around that factory changed the face of labor. Prior to the advent of machines, the production of goods—from the spinning of yarn to the fabrication of a musket—was a time-consuming, painstaking indi-

Mass production in a shirt factory: as the Industrial Revolution progressed, the factory began to replace the home as the focus of everyday life.

vidual effort conducted by skilled craftspeople, most often at home. When you bought anything—from a shirt to a weapon—you could usually be sure of two things: Someone had put a lot of time and effort into your purchase and there was no other exactly like it in the world. (In a nineteenth-century Italian children's story, the woodworker Gepetto so lovingly crafts Pinocchio that the puppet comes to life. Today, Gepetto would simply be Inspector No. 17 at a company cranking out *Pinocchio* videotapes.) As factories began churning out identical goods in unheard-of numbers, labor was reduced to performing routine tasks organized around those machines. Raw materials, machines, and people in turn became interchangeable parts in a great industrial engine. In the early nineteenth century that industrial engine produced the most enduring symbol of the industrial revolution (besides soot): the railroad.

THEY WERE RAILROADED!

In 1825 the first railroad began carrying coal from Darlington to the port of Liverpool, twenty-five miles away. Four years later, George and Robert Stephenson's "Rocket," their locomotive upgrade, attained the remarkable speed of 29 mph. After that demonstration of feasibility, steam engines were rapidly manufactured in quantity, despite the occasional glitch—exploding, jumping the tracks, or simply colliding head-on. You might miss the train in those days, but you couldn't miss its terrific potential.

Soot 'r' us.

The railroad was an enterprise unlike anything ever seen. It used unheard-of quantities of raw materials—coal, steel, lumber—and spurred those industries to further expansion. It consumed huge sums of capital, capital that, fortunately, had been generated by earlier industrialization in manufacturing. It required tremendous numbers of laborers, from track layers to conductors, ticket-takers to engineers, laborers made available by a spurt in population growth.

The railroad—both child and benefactor of the Industrial Revolution—was the origin of another of our modern landmarks: the corporation. A refinement of the joint stock company, the corporation became the institutional means to raise the huge sums of money needed to run a railroad and the organizational system by which it could be efficiently administered. Corporations soon were identified by the abbreviations and initials trailing after company names: Inc. (American), Limited (English), S.A. (French), and A.G. (German). Short though they were, these identifiers stood for the same thing. By stock issuance and through the principle of limited liability (the loss of the investment only, not the shirt as well), the corporation raised capital. Paper stock, as livestock before it, became a commodity of exchange.

The railroad spurred industrialization and carried it west, eventually linking all of Europe. Track was laid across rivers and gorges, tunnels blasted through the Alps. In 1860 the British went so far as to lay railway tracks underground, and three years later the first subway opened in London. Newspapers, consumer goods, and mail were now all delivered nationally by train. Vacationers could leave London for the beach at Brighton and return in one day (hence, they were known as "daytrippers"). The railroad made the transport of gold bullion easier and safer, which naturally resulted in England's first Great Train Robbery in 1857. By 1870, when General Helmuth von Moltke used the railroad to swiftly mobilize Prussian troops against France, over 100,000 miles of track had been laid across Europe.

A massive collection of rails, roadbeds, rolling stock, large terminals, small stations, timetables, restaurants and dining cars, the railroads showcased the improvements of technology and carried those improvements into new territory.

MORE, MORE, MORE

The railroad marked the beginning of a European love affair with technology that lasted until World War I, when technological progress turned from toasters to tanks. Every day seemed to bring another awesome technological achievement, such as the 1869 opening of the Suez Canal, whose one hundred-mile length shaved a good 4,000 miles off the ocean trip from India to Great Britain. Each innovation, from the Bessemer steel-making process to canned food, was broadcast to the world via telegraph, the news disseminated by papers cranked out on brand-new rotary printing presses. The Great London Exhibition of 1851, the first world's fair, was a hugely successful celebration of industrial progress; its iron and glass symbol, the Crystal Palace, was a triumph of prefabrication. Designed by Sir Joseph Paxton, the Crystal Palace resembled a huge greenhouse—no accident, considering that Paxton was also a horticulturalist. The Palace—all 1,851 feet of it, one foot for every year A.D.—housed the entire exhibition. Afterwards, the whole thing was taken apart, moved, and reassembled just outside London.

Other exhibitions followed in Paris, Vienna, and New York, each striving to outdo its predecessors in size, scope, and attendance. Technology, which had spawned mass production, now inspired the mass production of exhibitions whose theme might as well have been "The Wonderful World of Mass Production."

The scales tipped in favor of quantity, not quality, as mass-produced goods competed for the attention

The pre-fab Crystal Palace was pretty fab.

of millions of consumers. The latter half of the century saw the introduction of concepts that are commonplace today, including:

- magazine and newspaper advertising,
- Christmas as a commercial holiday (yes, Virginia, there once was no Santa Claus),
- the department store—the first one, in Paris, was called *Bon Marché,* which is French for "good buy." (And you thought the French had no sense of humor.)

For better or worse, there was simply more of everything. There was *so much* more that naturally someone got the bright idea of counting everything, which is how we know that:

- London, with a population of 988,000 in 1800, grew to 2,363,000 by 1851;

- the Belgians began building railroads in 1835; by 1870 they had 3,000 kilometers of rails completed;
- the number of letters carried in France grew from 64 million in 1830 to 358 million in 1869;
- circulation of *The Times* of London went from 5,000 a day in 1815 to 51,468 in 1854;
- the Parisian newspaper *Le Petit Journal* sold 212,500 papers daily in 1872 (without *Garfield*);
- Samuel Smiles's book *Self-Help,* which had sold 20,000 copies in the year of its publication (1859) sold 150,000 copies in 1889 and was by then translated into seventeen languages.

The most dramatic numerical change was in population. The Continental population grew from 190 million in 1800 to 295 million in 1870. Equally significant, demographers calculate that about five out of every seven persons born in Europe in the last two decades of this time period migrated to the cities.

BOOM TOWN

The character of cities underwent a startling change during the nineteenth century. The railroad station replaced the cathedral as the center of urban activity, as "all aboard!" overshadowed "praise the Lord."

The Industrial Revolution shifted the focus of economic and social life to the cities. Businesses, factories, schools, clubs, hospitals, and parks found themselves competing for suddenly limited urban real estate. Rising property prices in major cities led to residential congestion. Builders, finding themselves short of square footage (sorry, make that "horizontally challenged") took greater advantage of vertical space. A new form of apartment, the tenement, made its debut. It was made profitable to the landlord, and uncomfortable to the tenant, by the dubious innovation of shared sidewalls, which allowed ventilation and light to come in only at front and back. Well into the late nineteenth century, water had to be carried up in buckets and "night soil" (the substance contained in the chamber pot) carried down. The latter, a major hygienic problem of urban congestion, was relieved by

MAKING A DIFFERENCE

In 1849, British mathematician Charles Babbage (1792–1871) completed his design for a "Difference Engine," a mechanical calculator accurate to 31 digits. The machine was so expensive, complex, and unwieldy, that it wasn't until 1991 that the engine was actually constructed. Built from Babbage's original drawings by a team from the British Science Museum, the engine is 11 feet long, 7 feet high, weighs three tons, and is operated by turning a crank hundreds, even thousands of times. It isn't just more precise than an abacus, but better exercise as well.

Babbage also designed a more versatile machine

MAKING A DIFFERENCE (*continued*) . . . .
with the ability not only to perform advanced mathe-
matical functions, but to store instructions, input,
and results on perforated cards. His "Analytical Engine" was never built, but is nevertheless recognized
as the forerunner of the electronic computer.

   Babbage's most practical invention, however, had
nothing to do with large numbers, and everything to
do with large cattle. He invented the cowcatcher,
the metal frame attached to locomotives that pushed
obstacles (such as errant cows) from the railroad
tracks.

the unhailed technological achievement of nineteenth-
century urban development: interior plumbing.

City planners, when they managed to control the
breakneck speed of urban expansion, instituted sector-
alization—that's *zoning,* to you and me—by intention-
ally dividing the city into a good and bad "side of
the tracks." On the one side they plunked factories,
slaughterhouses, shipyards, and lower-class housing.
On the other side things were rather different: Fashionable residential and shopping districts enjoyed
paved streets and sidewalks, benefiting from the curb-
ing or removal of domestic and farm animals that
once roamed the streets. There were fine townhouses,
graciously proportioned parks, and well-paced and
level streets, illuminated by gas lamps.

The English, ever on the cutting edge of class division, soon added a new urban form: the suburb. The
first such development of note was Clapham, a few

miles out of London at the time (with Clapham Junction later to be a major intersection of railroad lines). By the turn of the nineteenth century it would be the residence of many of London's merchants.

The English were also proud pioneers of urban blight, as millions migrating to work in city factories found lodging in hastily built industrial towns. Charles Dickens gave the imaginary name "Coketown" to one such city in his novel *Hard Times* (1854):

> It was a town of red brick, or brick that would have been red if the smoke and ashes had allowed it. . . . It was a town of machinery and tall chimneys. . . . It contained several large streets all very like one another, and many small streets still more like one another, inhabited by people equally like one another.

Coke, a residue of burnt coal, was a crucial element in steel-making—therefore, more important than anything like fresh air. Besides, only the poor laborers lived anywhere near the coke furnaces. Factory managers and owners could afford to live elsewhere.

A decade prior to the publication of *Hard Times,* the nonfiction *Conditions of the Working Class* had appeared in England. Written by the German-born manager of a Manchester cotton business, this study detailed the evils inherent in the capitalist system. The recognition of those evils didn't prevent the book's author, Friedrich Engels (1820–1895), from prospering at his job. After all, he had a wife to support, as

---

BOW STREET BLUES

The growth of cities provided expanded economic opportunity for criminals, as well—all those potential victims in one place. In early nineteenth-century London, the only patrolmen were a collection of pensioners known as watchmen, who could be counted on to do exactly that when they encountered crime. In fact, more watchmen became either criminals or victims than protectors.

In 1829 British Home Secretary Sir Robert Peel established the first Metropolitan Police Force. Nicknamed both "Peelers" or "Bobbies" in honor (or ridicule) of their founder, equipped only with a whistle and a club labeled "Police Officer" (which most of them couldn't read), the police were a great success, driving much of the criminal population out of London—to outlying towns and boroughs, who soon found it necessary to organize their own police forces, which they naturally modeled after London's.

---

well as a perpetually starving friend: a German historian by the name of Karl Marx.

JUST DOWN THE STREET: CLASS CONFLICT

The son of a German lawyer, educated in philosophy and law, Karl Marx (1818–1883) specialized in two pursuits: philosophy and getting chased out of town. He was thrown out of Cologne, Germany, in 1842,

Karl Marx knew all the Engels.

when his work as a newspaper editor proved too radical for the local authorities. He traveled to Paris and within three years was asked to leave by the Parisian authorities. (He returned a few years later to make sure they really didn't want him around, and they ran him out again.)

After briefing Engels in Paris in 1842, Marx accompanied him on a guided tour of working life in industrial England. Throughout the countryside, men, women, and children worked endless hours for minuscule wages, struggling to survive in identical company towns.

The harshness of that working life had been responsible for the mid-nineteenth-century emergence of trade unions, and the late-nineteenth-century appearance of labor unions. The objectives of these pressure groups ranged from demands for higher wages and shorter working hours to a radical change in government. The English government, perhaps more advanced and certainly more worried than most, passed the Factory Act of 1833, which compassionately restricted labor for children under 13 to nine hours a day. A later act, in 1847, reduced the work day to ten hours for boys under 18, as well as for women.

To Marx, such reform was next to useless. True change would come about not as a result of well-meaning tinkering but through revolution. He saw capitalism itself as a dreadfully exploitive economic system that flowed on the sweat of the workers—one that would inevitably fall before the historical might of the working class.

Marx explained the inherent flaw in the capitalist system: Capitalism, of course, was based on profit. But, he argued, all things being equal—the cost of raw materials, equipment and factories, labor, and management—the price of any given item should simply equal the cost of its production. According to this theory, business should always break even. This led to the Big Question: Where did *profit* come from? If business owners were reaping a profit—and they obviously were—somebody else was reaping the shaft. Marx concluded that the entrepreneur was paying his workers less than the value of their labor and pocketing the difference. (Evidently Marx rejected the idea that an entrepreneur would ever make the consumer pay

SUFFERING, NOT SUFFRAGE

As early as 1792, Mary Wollstonecraft's (1759–1797) *A Vindication of the Rights of Women* made the case for equality of the sexes. Its appearance in England caused not a political outcry but a thud. The Enlightenment might have opened people's eyes to the idea that "all men are created equal," but the blinders stayed on when it came to women. It took the Industrial Revolution to provide the opportunity for any real advancement. Industry, its focus on efficient production, saw women not as domestic dependents but as potential labor. Their entry into the paid labor force proved that they could be exploited just as badly as men. Worse, in fact. Working women might be equal to men in the eyes of industry, but they were still paid by men—and paid according to their inferior social and political status.

As for the right to vote, even in politically progressive England, with the support of the Chartist movement (see Chapter 2) and the endorsement of British economist and philosopher John Stuart Mill (1806–1873), women's suffrage came only in 1918. (Of course, it could have been worse: Suffrage wasn't extended to Swiss women until 1971.)

more than an item was worth. He'd obviously never seen a Pet Rock.) The essence of this "capitalist conspiracy," put simply, is that labor is exploited in order to generate profit and property. Marx's contemporary, the French socialist Pierre-Joseph Poudhon (1809–1865) loudly exclaimed: "Property is theft," in *What Is Property?* (copyright 1840).

In his famous polemic, *The Communist Manifesto* (1848) co-authored with Engels, Marx outlined a theory of history which posited class conflict as the continuing engine of change. Tension between any dominant class and the oppressed classes would always reach a point of conflict, at which time the dominant class would be displaced or overthrown. The bourgeoisie, oppressed in the eighteenth century, had overthrown the aristocracy, only to become the oppressors of the working class, or proletariat. *The Communist Manifesto,* urging the proletariat to overthrow the bourgeois capitalists, ends with the charge: "Workers of the world, unite! You have nothing to lose but your chains."

It had both a conspiratorial element (the there-he-is-get-him approach to human behavior) and a soothing element of victimization (the woe-is-me reduction of complicated conditions to a simplistic relationship between exploiter and exploited).

Marx believed that, as Newton had discovered the fundamental laws of physics, he had discovered the fundamental laws of history. And his ideas sold. His was to become the most powerful ideology of the modern world, as Lenin, Stalin, Mao, and Castro all became K. Marx shoppers.

Marx was a close observer of his time, a fact that quickly made his theory dated. As the century progressed, social conditions improved—slowly, but perceptibly. The imminent, inevitable overthrow of the bourgeoisie never materialized. What emerged, some thirty years after his death, was not class war but world war.

SUMMARY

The period between 1815 and 1848 was one of political unrest and revolution, as political freedom and constitutional representation struggled against reactionary, absolutist rule.

The development of nationalism culminated in the unification of Germany and Italy.

The Industrial Revolution changed European social and economic life, as factories with steam-operated machinery employed large numbers of workers and produced large quantities of consumer goods. The industrial city was a bleak, polluted place in which workers led cramped, unsanitary lives.

A major and persistent trend was a population shift from the countryside to the city. Europe was becoming an urban place.

Rapid industrial progress, confidence in technology, and the surge of nationalism proved an intoxicating mixture for Europe's major powers. In the coming decades, the resulting international competition would send them reeling toward one heck of a bar fight.

CHAPTER 3

NATIONAL COMPETITION AND OVERSEAS EXPANSION
(1870–1914)

YOU MUST REMEMBER THIS

Europe's nations, in the vanguard of technological progress and military power, went on a global spree of empire building to satisfy their appetite for economic expansion, strategic strength, and national prestige. Friction generated by the scramble for territory in Africa, Asia, and the Pacific was reflected on the Continent, where rampant militarism escalated into a contest for the title of "The Greatest"—a competition that led Europe to the brink of war.

IMPORTANT EVENTS

★ Creation of the German Empire, 1871

★ Establishment of the Dual Alliance, 1879

★ Establishment of a French protectorate in Tunisia, 1881

★ Establishment of British domination of Egypt, 1882

★ Construction of the first gasoline-powered automobile by Karl Benz, 1885

★ Publication of Sigmund Freud's first major work, *The Interpretation of Dreams*, 1899

★ Sinking of the world's largest ocean liner, *Titanic*, on its maiden voyage, 1912

★ Balkan Wars, 1912–1913

In the four decades preceding the outbreak of World War I (1914), Europe stood at the peak of its power and influence. It dominated the world by every statistical measure, from GNP to size of standing armies. European steamship lines dominated the world's sea lanes; the English built battleships for the Japanese, and the Germans trained the Turkish army. Nationalism flourished, then overran Europe as countries competed for the title of "Big Man on Continent."

Yet while confidence in technology continued, these years were marked by a deepening doubt in reason. There were disturbing indications in science, art, and politics that—contrary to Enlightenment thought—individuals were unable to master even themselves, let alone an increasingly complex universe. The doubt in reason seemed justified when in 1914 the very system set up to safeguard peace in Europe all but guaranteed war.

WORLD WIDE WEB

Germany had come far since serving as Napoleon's personal punching bag at the start of the century. When Germany defeated France in 1870 to complete Bismarck's dream of unification, it became the commanding presence on the Continent. Germany's army, population, and university system were the envy of Western Europe, its industrial progress—fueled by the rich resources of the Ruhr and Saar valleys—unrivaled anywhere in the world. In 1897, when the German

**WHO'S
H
O**
☛

You Get the Picture

By the late nineteenth century, portraits of European bigwigs included photographs as well as paintings. Motion pictures were already being made. There even exists scant footage of the aging Queen Victoria—and a good deal more of Kaiser William II of Germany, the first known movie ham. You can find pictures of everyone below (no autographs, please):

Kaiser William II (1859–1941): The most significant monarch of his time—vain and pretentious; he led Germany into World War I.

Nicholas II (1868–1918): Russian czar, absolutist to the rather sudden end of his days.

Sigmund Freud (1856–1939): Viennese physician and couch potato who developed psychoanalysis.

Cecil Rhodes (1853–1902): Successful gold and diamond miner, great exponent of British imperialism, who got Rhodesia (Zimbabwe) named after him.

Rudyard Kipling (1865–1936): Nobel Prize–winning author (1907) who celebrated empire, coining the famous phrase "white man's burden."

Sarah Bernhardt (1844–1923): French actress, known the world over for her dramatic interpretations and flamboyant style.

foreign minister, Prince Bernard von Bülow (1849–1929), said that Germany wanted "a place in the sun," it wasn't wishful thinking, but an announcement that Germany intended to throw its considerable weight around.

Having unified Germany, Chancellor Otto von Bismarck now sought to secure its permanence as the arbiter of Continental affairs. Through a vigorous and pragmatic diplomacy known as *Realpolitik,* Bismarck accomplished two goals vital to Germany's security: the maintenance of a new balance of power in Europe and the isolation of Germany's time-honored rival, France.

Bismarck's first move was the Dual Alliance of 1879, a mutual defense arrangement linking Germany with Austria. This alliance ensured that, should France commit an act of aggression against one, the other would provide assistance. Next, in 1882, he negotiated the Triple Alliance, which bound Italy, Germany, and Austria in a similar agreement. To reassure Russia as to his peaceful intentions, Bismarck then drew that country into an 1887 Reinsurance Treaty. Good for a three-year period, the treaty stipulated that Germany would not back Austria if Austria decided to attack Russia. At the same time, he managed to maintain cordial relations with Great Britain.

Bismarck's network of alliances assured Continental stability and prevented France from strengthening her own hand through alliance. The only problem with his plan was that it required Bismarck to look after it. Unfortunately, in 1890 he was dismissed by Kaiser William II, who intended to personally handle Germany's foreign policy.

Kaiser William II failed to grasp the intricacies of Bismarck's careful diplomacy.

Manhandle is more like it. The first thing Kaiser William II did was fail to renew Germany's Reinsurance Treaty with Russia. Allowing this treaty to lapse left a free spot on Russia's dance card. France, out in the diplomatic cold, was more than happy to cut in. Between 1894 and 1895 the French created something of a diplomatic revolution by concluding an alliance with Russia, thus binding the country with the most radical tradition and the nation with the most conservative one—across and against Germany. The French then turned around and made nice with the English. *Entente Cordiale,* or "cordial understanding," in 1904 resolved colonial differences and brought England down from the heights of its "splendid isolation," a policy of non-alignment in Europe.

THOSE GRANDCHILDREN!

The children of Queen Victoria (she had four sons and five daughters) followed royal marital practices that made much of European monarchy blood related. Victoria was grandmother to Kaiser William II (r. 1888–1918) of Germany and to the wife (Czarina Alexandra) of Czar Nicholas II of Russia (r. 1894–1917). Her own English grandchild was King George V (r. 1910–1936), which meant that all three of these grandchildren would be heading warring nations after 1914. So much for the reunion barbecue.

Queen Victoria (1819–1901) ruled England for 63 years, the longest reign of any English monarch. She seemed the very incarnation of the British Empire: staid, patriotic, conservative, dependable, and durable.

Bismarck had feared what he called "a nightmare of coalitions." (He should talk—he started it all.) That nightmare finally came to pass when in 1907 Russia entered into an understanding with Great Britain similar to that country's *Entente Cordiale* with France. This firmed up the contestants in the latest edition of "European Feud"—Germany, Austria, and Italy, playing for the *Triple Alliance,* versus Great Britain, France, and Russia, playing for the *Triple Entente.*

Bismarck's alliance system, a complex web of political relationships, thus degenerated into an international face-off that served only to heighten tension. The confrontational aspect wasn't lost on Europe's military leaders, who began drawing up plans for wars that would lead their nations to greater glory.

LET'S GET READY TO RUMBLE!

As military strategists designed plans around the alliance system, they were sure that whatever the future war would be, it would be swift, intense, and over very quickly. Few, if anyone, imagined that the modern industrial state, with its finely tuned financial system and extensive international trade, could endure a long war—any state would be ruined by it. In popular German thought, no matter who fought for what reason, it would be a *frischer und fröhlicher Krieg,* a "fresh and joyous war."

Such thinking was simply wrong, as two world wars have subtly suggested.

The spirit of the times focused on constructive opportunity, not destructive capability. For those of fighting age, war stood for gallant and heroic action, national pride and camaraderie, daring campaigns carried out with dash and verve. The young heroes in Eric Remarque's famous war novel, *All Quiet on the Western Front* (1930), are taught in school that they are the "iron youth"—a commonplace metaphor for youthful invincibility. Lightning cavalry charges thundered through the dreams of English aristocrats, continuing the tradition of Alfred Lord Tennyson's 1854 poem, *The Charge of the Light Brigade*—an upbeat commentary on a sheerly stupid and costly military action in the Crimean War (which was fought in Chapter 2). Victory would be glorious; death, heroic; great deeds, commemorated. Young men looked forward to war as if it were Mortal Kombat, not grim reality.

It was perhaps the last time anyone could look at war as a romantic escapade. The same technology that made mass production possible would do no less for mass destruction. War, when it came, would decimate a generation of European youth, their dreams of victory and glory dying miserably and mud caked.

Yet military strategists, aware that the wars of national unification had been over in weeks (seven weeks in Germany's case, as we saw in the last chapter) and ignoring the lessons of that lengthy American tragedy, the Civil War, drooled over war plans that emphasized attack—the quick and decisive offensive against the enemy. The most famous of such plans bears its originator's name, General Alfred von Schlieffen (1833–1913).

The Schlieffen Plan, crafted in 1905, was designed to quickly knock France out of the action, while directing a holding action against Russia. A shortcut through neutral Belgium, a quick march through northern France, and the German army would reach Paris within weeks. By the time Russia could mobilize in support of France, the German army would already

MAYBE SOMEONE SHOULD WRITE "ON PEACE"

The guru of military strategists was Prussian officer Karl von Clausewitz (1780–1831), of whom it has been rightfully said that he wrote the book on war. He studied military strategy in the best school—the Napoleonic Wars. After a rich wartime career (he fought at Waterloo and even served time as a French prisoner of war), he taught at the Prussian military academy. In his three-volume work *On War* (1833), published after his death, he argued that war was simply another tool of state policy—like diplomacy, but with louder parties. He influenced generations of military strategists with the assertion that moderation in war was an absurdity—that once declared, its aims must be the destruction of the enemy's ability to resist. This was interpreted as a justification for a chilling new idea: "total war," which sought not just specific military goals but also the annihilation of an opponent.

Of course, this was well before the annihilation of the enemy could be accomplished by the push of a button.

have been redirected—thanks to the railroad system— to the east.

Less renowned than the Schlieffen Plan is the French Plan, which was to have a bunch of different plans. Plan No. XVII, like the Schlieffen Plan, also called for a lightning offensive. It was designed to quickly regain the provinces of Alsace-Lorraine, territories France had lost to Germany in 1870.

Count Alfred von Schlieffen: A man with a plan.

Such offensive plans demanded preparedness, which in turn demanded men and weapons. By the end of the century, every major European country had peacetime conscription. There were 400,000 men in arms in Germany; 350,000, in France. Governments paired off with armament manufacturers to ensure that they kept up with the latest in military technology. (The German Krupp family rose to world prominence supplying armaments first to Prussia, then to Germany.) The constant clamor for more, newer, and better weapons furthered the careers of men like Sir Basil Zaharoff (1850–1936), arms salesman to the world,

who was known, because of his cheerful warmonger-
ing, as the "merchant of death." (He was later
knighted for guessing the winning side in World
War I.)

WHEN DO WE GET TO THE "PEACE" PART?

The Hague Peace Conferences were two conferences
held in the Netherlands in 1899 and 1907. Dedicated
to preserving peace in the face of the continuing
arms buildup, the participants mostly drew up new
rules on how to make war. In particular, the conferences agreed to forbid aerial bombing and the use of
poison gas, both of which would make their debut
anyway in the coming war.

The height of this military buildup came when German Emperor William II ("Kaiser Bill" to you and
me) decided that he wanted more than soldiers. He
wanted boats, too—great big ones. In 1897 he agreed
to a mammoth naval-building program proposed by
Admiral Alfred von Tirpitz. The British realized that
the German naval buildup was hardly designed with
France, Russia, or Austria in mind. In 1905 they responded with their own new navel program, launching
the first of a new battleship series: HMS *Dreadnought.*
Other ships followed quickly, inspiring and irritating
the Germans into building more and bigger ones of
their own. This "naval race" added to the frightening
prospect of war.

MY MOTHER WEARS
COMBAT BOOTS

These alliances and military buildups reflect the growth of rivalry and the intensity of nationalism among the so-called "Great Powers." Each nation competed for "Best Armed," "Most Industrial," "Gaudiest Uniform," "Greatest Pretension," and "Hokiest Mythical Ancestor." All of that stuff—cannon wadding, uniforms, flags, medals—can be subsumed under the expression *jingoism*, which originated with a bit of lesser English poetry (from the *In-Your-Face* School of Literature):

> We don't want to fight but, by
>   jingo, if we do,
> We've got the ships, we've got the
>   men, we've got the money, too.

Every major European country had outspoken commentators trumpeting war as a manly art. In the military-industrial metaphor of the day, war was the fire that tempered the steel of the nation. General Robert S. S. Baden-Powell (1857–1941), the Englishman who founded the Boy Scouts, once remarked that of all sports, manhunting was the most enjoyable. Baden-Powell also introduced the concentration camp to humanity, during the Boer War of 1899–1902 in South Africa. (This was before *reverent* replaced *bloodthirsty* in the Boy Scouts' motto.)

Jingoism wasn't only the most belligerent nineteenth-century ideology; it was also the most creative.

It inspired the wholesale manufacture of noble ancestors (generals all, making glorious and bloody sacrifices in the name of the homeland), a reverence for the "sacred soil" of the nation (frequently seized from a neighboring state), and a chauvinistic lyricism about national language and culture (the English made

CLOTHES MAKE THE MAN

The period's reverence for all things military reached its zenith in 1906, when a captain of the Prussian Guards marched into the town of Köpenick, Germany, with a contingent of soldiers in tow. He arrested Köpenick's mayor and treasurer on the grounds of financial malfeasance. After directing the police chief to ensure order in the town while he completed his mission, the captain collected the town's accounting records—and 4,000 marks. After ordering his men to escort the mayor and treasurer to nearby Berlin for interrogation, the captain left alone—with all of the money.

The captain of the Prussian Guards was a shoemaker named William Voigt. He had bought the uniform at a second-hand store in Berlin. After donning it, he had simply commandeered a group of soldiers out in the street and set off for Köpenick. His capture and subsequent trial became the subject of worldwide editorials, songs, cartoons—even an opera. After a brief stay in prison, he went on an extended personal appearance tour.

Everyone got a good laugh out of the German impostor whose orders were blindly followed, simply because he was wearing a uniform.

Shakespeare a national hero, as the French did with Joan of Arc; the Germans celebrated Wagnerian myths, music, and prejudice).

Nationalism produced a Continental race for superlatives. An Englishman wrote a book entitled *Greater Britain,* and some Frenchman started speaking of "Greater France." Greater meant bigger. Here in the more commercially minded U.S., we had the Great Atlantic and Pacific Tea Company. (Great though it was, it was also too long and soon became known simply as the A&P.) The U.S. also saw its own version of unification, when P. T. Barnum's "Greatest Show on Earth" merged with James Bailey's show in 1881. Finally, the *Titanic* was launched in 1911 as the "Greatest Ship Ever Built" and in 1912 ran into the "Greatest Iceberg Ever Seen."

That sinking feeling: After the Titanic *sank on its maiden voyage in 1912, one of its surviving officers later said he was never confident again.*

Naturally, if your country was greater, some other country had to be less great. By the same token, the people of your country were better. But better than who? And on what grounds? The nationalistic emphasis on distinctive ethnic qualities led to some fateful, wrong-headed, and ultimately tragic answers. France's Arthur de Gobineau (1816–1882), in *The Inequality of the Human Races* (1853–1855), argued that the predominant issue in politics was race—and that the Aryan race was superior. Houston Stewart Chamberlain (1855–1927), the English son-in-law of the great German opera composer Richard Wagner (1813–1883), in *Foundations of the Nineteenth Century* (1900) specifically glorified the Germans as Aryans who were "pre-eminent" among all of humankind.

The equation for racial superiority demanded an inferior race and for much of nineteenth-century Europe that meant the Jews. Although the term "anti-Semitic" had been coined during the nineteenth century, this prejudice had a long European history; now there came a renewed surge of anti-Semitism. In Russia the czarist regime instituted a relentless series of officially sanctioned military raids on Jews, known as pogroms. France was torn apart by it; the Dreyfus Case (1894–1906) rocked France for years.

DREYFUS

The Dreyfus Affair shook the very foundations of French government. Alfred Dreyfus, an officer in the French army, was accused of attempting to pass secrets to Germany. It was assumed that Dreyfus, being a Jew,

Guilty until proved innocent: Alfred Dreyfus.

was likely to be disloyal to the army. He was found guilty of treason in 1894 and sentenced to life imprisonment. His conviction provided anti-Semites with ammunition for their propagandist tracts—and further cemented prejudice within the French army.

Two years later, evidence came to light that exposed the traitor as a Major Esterhazy. Embarrassed, the army had to try Esterhazy, but managed to come up with enough forged evidence to acquit him. French author Émile Zola, in response to the acquittal, published a fiery denunciation of the authorities—*J'Accuse.* It aroused public outrage over both the original injustice and the army's willful cover-up of its mistake. In 1898, after an officer confessed to having forged the evidence against Dreyfus, Esterhazy was thrown out of the army and left France.

In 1899 a Court of Appeal ordered a new trial for Dreyfus. Incredibly, it again found Dreyfus guilty but

FRANCE'S DELICATE CONDITION

The Third Republic, shaken by the Dreyfus Affair, had never been that strong to begin with. After Napoleon III's surrender to Prussian forces in 1870, French republicans had proclaimed the establishment of a provisional Third Republic. But even before the fighting with Prussia had ended, it was in trouble—what with two kinds of monarchists (Bourbon and Orleans), socialists, anarchists, and the occasional Bonapartist (Prince Napoleon, another nephew of Napoleon I) running around.

In March 1871 a group of socialists seized control of the French capital, drove the republican government out of the city, and established the Commune of Paris. The Communards, ruling by municipal council, began to enact socialist reforms, but by the start of April republican forces returned to take back the city. The battle for Paris was both brief and savage. The Communards, who suffered almost 20,000 casualties, burned much of the city. On May 28 the Commune fell.

It wasn't until 1875 that the Third Republic had a constitution, and even then movements to restore some kind of monarchy still kept popping up. As late as 1887, the republic was threatened by General Georges Boulanger (1837–1891)—French war minister, hero of the Franco-Prussian War, and no fan of

FRANCE'S DELICATE CONDITION
(*continued*)
. . . .
the republic. Supported by both monarchists and Bonapartists, Boulanger appeared on the verge of duplicating the coup d'etat of an earlier French general—Napoleon Bonaparte. But when his republican opponents in the government charged him with plotting to overthrow the government, Boulanger proved he was no Napoleon. His nerve failed him and he fled to Belgium, where he took his own life in 1891.

generously shortened his sentence to ten years of imprisonment. An enraged public swept the government out of office. The new government quickly pardoned Dreyfus—a shrewd move, since Esterhazy had confessed to having been the traitor. Dreyfus received the Legion of Honor and reinstatement with the rank of major, and he served in the First World War.

Not surprisingly, as it dragged on, the Dreyfus case became a political football. Supporting the conviction proved costly to the army, now exposed as racist; to the government, removed for condoning an injustice; and to the Catholic Church. The Church, as a State-subsidized organization, had supported the army right down the line. And in 1905 it paid for that support when legislation provided for the legal separation of Church and State.

In reaction particularly to the horror of the Dreyfus Affair, and to the anti-Semitism sweeping Europe, Viennese journalist Theodor Herzl (1860–1904) began the call for the establishment of a Jewish state. As the founder of the Zionist movement, he began a long struggle for the Jewish homeland that culminated in the establishment of Israel (1947)—a scrap of real estate on a continent that, in the late nineteenth century, the European nations were treating as their own backyard.

PLUNDER AND REIGN

The four decades between 1870 and 1914 witnessed Europe's love affair with imperialism—a policy best described as "throwing your nation's weight around." Easily and joyfully equating technological advantage with moral superiority, the European powers sought to spread their influence throughout the "backward" countries of the world—at the point of a machine gun, if necessary (and it often was). But it was worth it to the high-minded Europeans. After all, behind that machine gun—in the home country—stretched railroads and factories, paved city streets and hospital corridors, grocery and library shelves—all the characteristics of a rational, orderly, industrial society. In the mind of imperialists, Europe was unquestionably advanced—indeed, the pinnacle of civilization—and therefore had both the right and the obligation to assist poor natives around the globe. This condescension is succinctly expressed in Rudyard Kipling's famous poem, "The White Man's Burden," in which the Englishman urged the United States to take up that "burden" in the Philippines after the Americans

*Rudyard Kipling
(1865–1936)
—defender of the
imperialist faith—
won the Nobel Prize
for Literature
in 1907.*

had annexed the islands in 1899. The white man's burden, apparently, was

> *To wait, in heavy harness
> On fluttered folk and wild—
> Your new-caught sullen peoples
> Half devil and half child.*

Imperialism was a mixed bag of high-sounding theories, crass intentions, stupid and mendacious acts, lots of little wars, much misery and some small hope for the natives—rather like network sweeps week. Yet it

THIS LAND IS MY LAND
· ·
How pervasive was European domination at the turn of
the century? Consider this: In 1908 Belgium, known to
us now as the home of Hercule Poirot, officially annexed what is now Zaire, naming it the Belgian Congo.
Belgium, at 12,000 square miles, is roughly the size
of Massachusetts. Zaire? At roughly 900,000 square
miles, it's four times the size of Texas.

enjoyed a brief heyday simply because Europe had the
firepower to back up its ideology. Guns prevailed over
spears, the telegraph over signal drums, the gunboat
over the war canoe—and so Europe prevailed over
the world.

If imperialism can be boiled down to "might makes
right," then its most significant feature, colonialism,
can best be described as "I got dibs on that." The
"Great" Powers gobbled up territory right and left—
often squabbling with one another over the same
countries, while indigenous peoples stood on the side-
lines awaiting the outcome. (In fact, when the European powers met in Berlin in 1898 to lay down the
ground rules for carving up Africa, no one from Africa
was even invited.) Between 1881, when the French established a protectorate over Tunisia (with the English
gaining control of Egypt in 1882), and 1912, when the
French established a protectorate over Morocco, Africa was chaotically annexed by the Europeans. Often
called the "Scramble for Africa" (an English politician compared it with a miner pegging out claims),

this frenzied landgrab brought all of Africa, except Liberia and Ethiopia, under European control.

The United States, eager to prove it too was now a world power, grabbed Hawaii in 1898 and placed the Philippines under American control following the Spanish-American War (1898). The English, Germans, and French lost no time going after islands in the Pacific. The French picked up Tahiti in 1880; the Germans gathered up over 200 islands at once and named it the Bismarck Archipelago; in 1884 Great Britain joined the club by annexing the part of New Guinea that the Germans hadn't.

Brutal magnanimity wasn't the only reason for European imperialism. Self-interest (surprise!) played a large part as well, as Europe looked to colonies for economic support. The last three decades of the nineteenth century saw a long depression in Europe, marked by intensifying national competition and widespread unemployment. Millions sought relief by emigrating to America. Those who remained talked about enacting protective tariffs—even in that sanctuary of free trade, England. The markets of Europe were becoming saturated; investors were faced with an excess of funds and a dearth of places to put it. Colonies provided new markets for the sale of national goods, as well as new raw materials needed to stoke the demanding industrial machine at home. Colonies also provided new opportunities for investment. Looking for a better return, European investors urged their states to expand into places where their capital could be profitably invested and secured.

In the eyes of European industry, imperialism was

a godsend. For Marxists, it was a necessary phase of capitalism. In his most influential tract, *Imperialism: The Highest Stage of Capitalism* (1917) V. I. Lenin (1870–1924)—the Russian revolutionary who eventually became the Soviet Union's first leader—explained that imperialism was simply a stay of execution for the doomed capitalist system. Faced with a surfeit of cash at home, capitalists were forced to expand their exploitation to new markets and lands.

Finally, there was a political element, an assumption that somehow the acquisition of colonies would assure continuing national greatness. (The common French expression for its colonial empire was *France d'Outre-Mer,* or "Overseas France.") As national rivalry grew in Europe, and as the United States grew in global significance, a colonial empire appeared to be a good bet on the future. (Heaven knows that when push comes to shove, having Tahiti on your side can make the difference between defeat and victory.) Great Britain proclaimed with pride and comfort that "the sun never sets on the British Empire." It was true. At the time, that empire stood at some 10 million square miles—about one-fifth of the earth's surface.

CALL ME BWANA

The "empire builders," as the colonists grandly styled themselves, were seen by the European public as magnificent benefactors: sun-burnished, lithe, doing good things for little people—like reducing them to racist stereotypes. Asians, in the colonial view, were often described as cunning; Africans, as child-like. It seems that along with technology, the Europeans were exporting their own brand of paternalistic racism. At its best, the colonists' behavior was ignorant and condescending, even if well-intentioned. (In our own country, William Howard Taft, governor of the Philippines before he became president, spoke of "our little brown brothers.") At its worst it was inhuman. Many colonial administrators acted with nothing but contempt for those they had subjugated, their views and behavior justified by moral superiority over these "primitive savages."

Such attitudes only made the wholesale exploitation of colonial resources and labor easier. After all, empire building was supposed to be a benefit to the national economy, not a financial strain ("empire on the cheap" was the English term). The social practices

Not much hope for these diamond miners.

WE'VE GOT TO GET OUT OF THIS PLACE

As European nations seized territory, many Europeans seized the opportunity to leave their homeland for greener pastures. Imperialists had hoped that people would resettle in the new territories. But let's face it—which would you rather do: live under the resentful hostility of oppressed natives in the Congo or move to Philadelphia? (Okay, how about San Francisco, then?)

Most emigrating Europeans did head for the United States, coming from two broad areas: from northern and western Europe in the 1880s and from southern and eastern Europe in the 1890s. In the year 1907 alone, 1,285,349 pairs of eyes saw the Statue of Liberty, a gift from the French commemorating the centennial of American Independence. (The British sent a toaster.)

The record number of immigrants inspired the steamship lines to build even bigger ships to profit from the new traffic in human cargo. The *Titanic* carried some 1,200 immigrants in steerage on its maiden voyage. (Few arrived and fewer got refunds.)

that followed are easily guessed, but difficult to really imagine. The colonies' chief economic element became labor—labor pitilessly directed toward digging gold or diamonds in South Africa, tapping rubber in the Congo, mining in Malaya, and harvesting peanuts and bananas in West Africa. Bodies were broken and health ruined in the construction of roads and ports, all in the name of export. After World War I started, fewer people were used up building roads—instead they were exported as army recruits.

Colonialism was hardly a one-way street, however. In return for the exploitation of their natural resources, natives received the benefits of European colonial administration: roads, hospitals, schools, and socks. If you were lucky, you could go to a colonial school as a kid and learn where Europe was. After a brief stint building a road, your health would be wrecked, so you'd spend some time in a colonial hospital, during which you'd decide to emigrate to Europe. Your son would grow up in Europe, return to the home country, raise an army, and throw the colonists out.

The colonial situation was relatively short-lived, dependent as it was on European arrogance, superior firepower, and economical administration. Colonial domination supplied native inhabitants with the tools to effect its demise: technology, education, and a terrific resentment for colonial oppressors.

NEVER-NEVER LAND

As all this empire building, military preparation, and flag waving was going on, J. M. Barrie's *Peter Pan* was being produced. It opened in London in 1904 and proved to be an enduring bit of fantasy, featuring Captain Hook, Peter, Wendy and the other Darling children. The play was an idealized portrait of the time: domestic bliss, solid finances, heavy banquets, and Sunday strolls in the park—all enjoyed by the middle and upper classes, whose servants shined silver and laid out several daily changes of clothes. This picture of inconsequential activity and ceremony marks the decade before and after the year 1900, a period known as the *Belle Epoque*—that beautiful time when Americans went to Europe for culture, Europeans went to the Riveria for pleasure, and the rest of the world went to hell in a handbasket.

For most of Europe the *epoque* was hardly *belle*. The business world was becoming truly global and as a result the European economy was badly unsettled. Industrial competition from the United States was intensifying. Agricultural competition from far-off places like Argentina and Australia was growing, as refrigerated ships allowed long-distance shipping of beef and mutton. An exponentially growing population increased both unemployment and social unrest.

Under such conditions, European political systems slowly moved beyond democracy as a political matter (the individual vote) to democracy as a social matter (the well-being of the citizenry). Socialism had grown to political prominence with the emergence of a number of national socialist parties toward the end of the century. Germany's Social Democratic Party, formed from two separate parties in 1875, would have the largest number of representatives in the lower house *(Reichstag)* of the German Parliament by 1912. The Labour Party was established in England in 1893, and the Social Democratic Workers Party formed in Russia in 1898. In France, several factions of Socialism joined in 1905 to form a united Socialist Party. Each of these parties (except Labour), while generally adhering to the Marxist theory of capitalism, modified Marxist strategy. That is, change was to occur not through revolution but reform, by parliamentary gains. The class struggle would be about votes, not guns.

Their effort was coincidental with the strides made by trade unions in the last three decades of the nineteenth century. Advances made in political reform had hardly altered the economic powerlessness of labor.

The arrest of a suffragette. In 1903 British suffragette Emmeline Pankhurst, dissatisfied with the women's suffrage movement's lack of progress, founded the Woman's Social and Political Union. The militant Union employed violent demonstrations, marches, hunger strikes, and arson to make its case. Although the new tactics made the Union the talk of the town, it wasn't until 25 years later that women got the vote.

Industry, not government, called the shots in the workers' daily lives. Trade unions had been organized to get immediate results in the workplace. Through their weapon of choice—the strike—unions sought better wages and improved working conditions. As the century drew to a close, unions increased the use of that weapon, expanding into general strikes—collective efforts to force not just a single employer's hand but governmental reform as well. Such strikes, which all failed but frightened governmental authorities, occurred in Belgium, Sweden, Spain, France, and the Netherlands in the decade before World War I.

At the start of the twentieth century a new element of social discontent emerged: the demand for the vote by women. The English Suffragette Movement, headed by Emmeline Pankhurst (1858–1928) who was joined by her two daughters and a sizable contingent of dissatisfied women, began in 1903 and sought by political persuasion to gain the vote. Nobody listened. Frustrated, the suffragettes started to burn buildings and throw bombs. *That* attracted attention. Arrested and cruelly force-fed when they refused to eat, Pankhurst, her daughters, and others raised the issue of the woman's vote to national prominence and lived to see their belated success when, after the war, "universal manhood suffrage" in Great Britain had the disqualifying middle term removed.

COOKING UP A STORM

Strikes and protests were on the rise in Russia as well as elsewhere. If the road to democracy had suddenly

V. I. Lenin (1870–1924), Russian revolutionary.

gotten rutted in Western Europe, in the east it was about to take a rather lengthy detour. By the late nineteenth century, Russia's autocratic, reactionary regime was beginning to show cracks. A major hint was the 1881 assassination of Czar Alexander II by a bomb-wielding revolutionary. Alexander II had introduced limited reform—the abolition of serfdom, for example—only as a grudging nod to economic necessity. He steadfastly refused, however, to have anything to do with constitutional measures. His son, Alexander III, wouldn't even nod. In the wake of his succession he reined in the populists, anarchists, nihilists, and reformers through censorship and harassment, and he began pogroms against the Jews. Assassins conspired to send him the way of his father but were arrested and executed in 1887.

One of the plotters was a man named Alexander Ulyanov, the son of a minor Russian official. His execution steered his younger brother, Vladimir Ilyich, toward Marxism. Vladimir's participation in St. Petersburg's revolutionary movement led to his arrest and exile in Siberia, where he took the name N. Lenin. (He is widely known by the combination of real and pen names: V. I. Lenin.) After his release in 1900, Lenin left Russia to assemble an organization of professional revolutionaries. But he would be back.

Back home, Alexander III spurred further industrialization and clamped down on intellectual groups and movements as Russia attempted to catch up with Western Europe. When he died in 1894 after a mere three-year reign, his son Nicholas II continued the Romanov recipe for disaster.

Ingredients:
- 1 Inflexible autocrat
- 1 Industrial program that brings people together in factories
- 1 War against the Japanese

Season with revolutionary exiles, Marxist tracts, and generic persecution.

Exploit people mercilessly.

Lose the war against the Japanese.

Yield: Big trouble.

Nicholas II's strident resistance to reform polarized the country. Throughout Europe it became generally

A FEW CRISES AND A COUPLE OF WARS

The turn of the century was beset with signs and acts of international disturbance. There were several colonial crises in Africa and Asia, all over territorial rights. Yet the four most significant wars of the time were severe challenges to European might, with two of them outrightly giving the lie to the myth of white supremacy. The Boer War in South Africa pitted the Boers—pastoral descendants of the early Dutch settlers—against recent British settlers. For nearly four years (1899–1902) they fought over land neither side had started with. After a series of embarrassing setbacks, the British finally staggered to victory.

More accurate harbingers of the imperial future were the Italo-Abyssinian War of 1895–1896 and the Russo-Japanese War of 1905–1906, in which people of color roundly defeated Europeans. The "white man's burden" was becoming burdensome indeed.

accepted that revolution was inevitable in Russia; the only debate was over the form and timing. After imperial troops fired on a group of protesters in January 1905—well, you could write the script by now—riots and general strikes followed, until the czar began constitutional reform. In this case, Nicholas created a Russian representative body called the Duma. Since Nicholas kept not just the veto power but also the right to dissolve the Duma whenever he wanted, all the first Duma could do was grouse. Nicholas then displayed his newfound sensitivity by dismissing the Duma for grousing too much. A second, third, and fourth Duma followed and disintegrated in much the same manner. This might have gone on until Dumasday, but World War I got in the way. At that point, there was no question of reasonable reform. Indeed, by then there was serious doubt as to the value of reason itself.

GOING, GOING, GONE

The long-held belief that reason prevailed in human thought and behavior, that there was a reasonable and knowable universe, began a slow fade at the turn of the century. It clearly wasn't reasonable for Prince Rudolph, the heir to Austria's Hapsburg throne, to commit suicide in his hunting lodge—and to be joined in the act by his mistress—sometime during the night of January 30–31, 1889. Neither was it reasonable for the decent, honorable scientist Dr. Henry Jekyll to discover that his psyche had a roommate—Mr. Edward Hyde—in Robert Louis Stevenson's short novel, *The Strange Case of Dr. Jekyll and Mr. Hyde* (1886). Nor did the Russian ballet star Vaslav Nijinsky follow proper form when he appeared to make love to a long scarf in Igor Stravinsky's famous ballet, *The Rites of Spring,* before an astounded Parisian audience in 1912.

Clearly, something was amiss. Here were indications of hidden forces within the human mind, forces untempered by reason. Vienna's Sigmund Freud attempted to observe and analyze these forces, offering a revolutionary explanation of irrational behavior. He posited the idea that what appears in the patient to be erratic and illogical actually has a particular origin in the individual's past. Some earlier experience had been repressed, perhaps a specific urge sublimated, only to resurface as irrational behavior. The human mind, that source of understanding and reason, was actually filled with repressive mechanisms, inaccessible fears, and unconscious desires. According to Freud, the mind was the scene of an ongoing conflict between ego (the part of us that recognizes and deals with reality) and the id (the beast in all of us).

Freud's focus on irrational behavior, hysteria, and the nature of dreams was reflected in the arts. In Jo-

Van Gogh's The Starry Night: *Painting by irrational numbers.*

seph Conrad's novel *Heart of Darkness* (1902), a Congo River journey into the depths of the jungle mirrored one character's descent into his own irrationality. Russian novelist Fyodor Dostoyevsky, in *Crime and Punishment* (1866) and *The Brothers Karamazov* (1880), examined madness, guilt, suffering, and the search for redemption in an imperfect world. Vincent Van Gogh's *The Starry Night* (1889), Edvard Munch's *The Scream* (1893), and Marcel Duchamp's *Nude Descending a Staircase* (1913) were celebrations of mood, emotion, and subjectivity—not reason.

These paintings, and others like them, joined the literary and philosophical movements that questioned traditional ideas about reason, time, and perception. After all, what had reliance on man's reason and ability produced but an industrial world in which machines prevailed over mankind, goods over goodness, production over propriety? Progress had given the world the transatlantic steamship, the Eiffel Tower, and good sewage. But it had also delivered the sixteen-hour workday, industrial accidents—and Jack the Ripper, the murderer of five prostitutes in 1888 London. Jack embodied the dark side of modern life. His surgical prowess indicated to many that he was the hidden, irrational side of a real-life Dr. Jekyll.

Even the physical sciences, which had produced the technology that had elevated Europe to pre-eminence, began to acknowledge fundamental flaws in their mechanistic outlook. In 1905 Albert Einstein (1879–1955) published three papers explaining his general theories of relativity. (The second of these papers contained his now-famous formula E = mc^2—energy equals the product of mass and the square of the speed of light.) Einstein's theory wasn't just scientifically sound but metaphysically explosive. Nothing, it seemed, was fixed, solid, or enduring. Distance was a variable. Even time was a variable. Enlightenment thinkers had set off in search of the fundamental laws of nature, confident that their discovery would lead to a rational, prosperous, enlightened society. The fruits of that search seemed to be saying that we could never fully understand, predict, or control either nature or ourselves. Indeed, how reasonable was it for one misadventure in a Balkan city to drag all of Europe into war?

A FINE MESS

The Balkan Peninsula continued to be a bone of contention among the European powers. The slow decline of the Ottoman Empire (the Turkish empire, its name derived from its thirteenth-century founder, Osman I) led to a European competition for dominance in the area, referred to as the "Eastern Question." If there had been an actual question, it probably would have been: "How can I get my hands on Ottoman territory while keeping everyone else's hands off?"

Russia had designs on anything that could be wrested from the weakening Turks—especially the straits leading from the Mediterranean to the Black Sea. Everyone else hated that idea. What—Russia wasn't big enough already? The conclusion of the Crimean War had left no one satisfied. In 1877 Russia went to war against the Turks again, beat them, and made satisfactory gains after forcing the Treaty of San Stefano (1878). Alas, Great Britain and Austria weren't happy, so they organized the Congress of Berlin that same year to resolve the issue. German Chancellor Bismarck, playing referee to France, Italy, Russia, Austria, Great Britain, and Germany, rewrote the Treaty of San Stefano so that *nobody* was happy. Perhaps least happy were the independence-minded Balkan countries of Bulgaria, Serbia, Montenegro, Macedonia, and Romania. They had no intention of helping to finally drive Turkish forces off their land only to see some other foreign power take their place.

The 1878 Treaty of Berlin wasn't an answer to the Eastern Question, but an equal distribution of dissatisfaction, which all but guaranteed further conflict. There were so many interested parties, all armed and looking for an opportunity for advancement, that anyone who felt like fighting could find a partner. Austria's annexation of Bosnia and Herzegovina was an idea whose time had not come and merely strengthened nationalist feeling there. The Turks warmed up for war against the Italians (1912) with a little civil war in 1911. The first of two Balkan Wars fought from 1912 to 1913 featured a coalition of Bulgaria, Serbia, Greece, and Montenegro fighting against the Turks. The second began once the Turks were defeated, and Serbia, Greece, and Montenegro turned to Bulgaria. The big winner was Serbia, who had been under Austria's thumb for some years. Now they were making threatening nationalist noises that disturbed the Austrians.

The Balkan fun might have gone on as it had for years—Balkan conflict, European interference, Turkish resistance, and treaties and conferences that resolved nothing—had the competition remained local. But nothing was local anymore. Disputes over territory ranged from Africa to Asia; shrinking markets heightened economic competition across the globe; and nationalist fervor demanded that countries prove their superiority with bigger, better, badder armies. With his intricate system of alliances, Bismarck had managed to maintain international stability, but after his dismissal by the Kaiser in 1890, that system proved a trap. With each international dispute there was less and less room to maneuver. After Austria's Archduke Ferdinand was assassinated by a Serbian nationalist in July 1914, giving Austria an excuse for reprisals against Serbia, the only maneuver left was war.

SUMMARY

Under Bismarck, the unified German empire grew to dominate Europe as a giant of industry, armament, and diplomacy, replacing France as "the straw that stirs the drink."

The alliance system, by which the major European states sought military support in anticipation of war, aggravated European politics and contributed to the likelihood of war in the decade before 1914.

Imperialism reached its zenith as the major European powers competed overseas for real estate, raw materials, markets, investment, and national prestige.

Social unrest and economic hardship contributed to the growth of national political parties.

Writers, artists, and philosophers focused on uncertainty and doubt as they moved away from notions of a reasonable universe. There was a growing realization of the influence of mood and personality on perception of reality. The individual was no longer seen as a detached analytical observer.

CHAPTER 4

A HALF CENTURY OF WARS
(1914–1945)

YOU MUST REMEMBER THIS

The first half of the twentieth century seemed to indicate the culmination of diplomatic, nationalistic, technological, and ideological progress was nothing more than total war. World War I (primarily a European conflict) and World War II (a global one, principally made so by Japan's participation) changed the face of world affairs. Two world wars effectively ended Europe's global domination as international affairs resolved themselves into a standoff between two superpowers—the Soviet Union and the United States.

IMPORTANT EVENTS

★ Outbreak of World War I, 1914

★ Armistice ending the fighting of World War I, 1918

★ Hitler becomes chancellor of Germany, 1933

★ Spanish Civil War, 1936–1939

★ Munich Pact and the culmination of appeasement, 1938

★ Outbreak of World War II when Germany attacks Poland, 1939

★ Japan attacks Pearl Harbor, 1941

★ The Battle of Stalingrad, the turning point in Europe, winter 1942–1943

★ V-E Day (Victory in Europe), May 7, 1945

THE WRONG TURN

World War I was kicked off by the chance encounter, on June 28, 1914, between two men on a Sarajevo street. The two men were the Archduke Francis Ferdinand, heir to the Hapsburg Austrian Empire, and Gavrilo Princip, a Serbian student and member of the nationalist Black Hand. Princip was having a cup of coffee in a cafe when the driver of the archduke's car, realizing he'd made a wrong turn, attempted to turn around in front of the cafe. Seeing this made-to-order opportunity, one which followed a botched assassination attempt by fellow Serbs that very morning, Princip dashed out of the cafe and fired his pistol at the archduke and his wife, mortally wounding them both.

Fateful motorcade, ca. 1914: the Archduke Ferdinand and his wife minutes before their assassination.

The assassination provided an opportunity for Austria to take harsh measures against Serbia, which had been stirring up opposition to Austrian policy in the Balkans, most notably Austria's seizure of Bosnia and Herzegovina in 1908. Austria issued a severe ultimatum to Serbia. The Serbian government complied with most of the demands, but not all. That was fine with Austria. All they really wanted was a good reason to fight. On July 28 Austria declared war against Serbia, a war it believed would be quick and local.

This action activated a series of alliance clauses that, within a week, brought every major European country into conflict. Here's the sequence of major events:

July 29:   Russia mobilizes in support of Serbia;

July 31:   Germany, allied with Austria, gives Russia an ultimatum to cease mobilization on its borders;

August 1:   Germans declare war on Russia;

August 3:   Germans declare war on France, allied with Great Britain;

August 4:   Great Britain declares war on Germany.

It was a week of confusion, fear, and excitement. Diplomacy was ineffective and hesitant. Heads of state were baffled. Army chiefs of staff were afraid not to mobilize lest they be caught off guard. The public, eager to see their boys make mincemeat of whoever it was they were going to fight, rejoiced at the news of impending campaigns. Never was a major war

WHO'S WHO

Dressed to the Nines and Armed to the Teeth

Uniforms were certainly popular during the first half of the twentieth century. Here's a list of some of the important figures of the time, with particular attention given to their outward appearance:

Woodrow Wilson (1856–1924): President of the United States during World War I and often adorned with the then height of fashion, the top hat.

V. I. Lenin (1870–1924): Leader of the new Soviet Union who sported a peak cap in good proletarian style.

Adolf Hitler (1889–1945): Dictator of Nazi Germany, usually dressed in a party (political, not birthday) outfit, with the Iron Cross he earned in World War I.

Benito Mussolini (1883–1945): Dictator of Fascist Italy and often in a black shirt, the color of his Fascist Party.

Joseph Stalin (1879–1953): Dictator of the Soviet Union, who donned a uniform in World War II when he assumed command of his country's armed forces.

Winston Churchill (1874–1960): Prime Minister of England during World War II who

WHO'S
H
O
☛

(*continued*)

most always wore a hat and occasionally wore a jumpsuit.

Franklin D. Roosevelt (1882–1945): President of the United States who never wore a uniform but did like to wear a cape.

begun so foolishly and greeted with such misplaced enthusiasm, as soldiers and generals alike told their families they'd be back within weeks.

No one in Europe seemed to recall General Sherman's line: "War is hell." However, everyone would soon learn what he was talking about.

Down in the Trenches

For a very short time, it looked as if the swift war everyone had anticipated would wrap itself up well before Christmas. Germany, following the Schlieffen Plan designed in 1905 by their former chief of staff, stormed through Holland and Belgium and deep into France in a matter of weeks, within fifty miles of the French capital. The German commander was General Helmuth von Moltke, nephew of the Helmuth von Moltke who had led the Prussians to quick victory against France in 1870 (see Chapter 2). Now he moved even more quickly than his uncle—too quickly, in fact. Believing the fall of Paris a done deal, he redirected troops to the southern front too soon—giving the French an opportunity to mobilize in defense of the capital.

Moltke's mistake was critical. A French general commandeered all the taxis of Paris (luckily, it wasn't raining or he never would have found any), packed them with soldiers, and rushed the lot off to the first Battle

*The German High Command ran roughshod
over the Low Countries.*

of the Marne (September 5–12, 1914), in northeastern France. This first use of motorized troop transport helped stem the German advance. The Germans, momentarily checked, attempted to go around the French lines by heading toward ports in the English Channel and North Sea. The French raced to prevent this, and the so-called "rush to the sea" ended in a stalemate, with two extended lines of troops facing one another. There was nothing to do but dig in.

None of the military strategists' plans covered this eventuality. Most prewar military scenarios, like the Schlieffen Plan, had been inspired by the genius of Napoleon Bonaparte, who had mastered Europe through the use of highly mobile forces. His divisions could take advantage of momentary cracks in the enemy's defenses, dart through openings, then wheel to attack before the enemy could react. The French emperor had rewritten the book on European warfare with his emphasis on speed, mobility, and modularity. But in the 500-mile-long face-off between World War I's opposing forces, there was no flank. There were no momentary cracks in the enemy wall; neither speed nor modularity mattered. The war, mapped out as a glorious and sudden charge, became linear and immobile.

Once it became apparent that both sides were going to have to fight from the temporary covering trenches they had dug, an entire new system of warfare developed. For the next four years soldiers would live in eight-foot trenches, supported through a maze of more trenches winding back to communications and supply lines. Each side would attempt to take the enemy trenches with a monotonously murderous sequence of events: first, an artillery barrage to soften up the enemy; then, an infantry charge toward the enemy in their trenches. As the advancing soldiers made their way through the territory between the two frontline trenches, they faced savage machine-gun fire and a barrage of cannon. Perhaps the enemy trench was taken; perhaps not. The devastated ground between the two front trench lines became known as "no man's land"—a still life of desolation pitted with shell holes, strung with barbed wire, and cluttered with corpses.

The terrible irony of the war is that going "over the

On charges across uncovered territory, soldiers faced relentless machine-gun fire, aerial strafing, land mines, and poison gas.

top" made very little difference in territory. At best, it moved the enemy lines back perhaps a few miles— a difference that would be made up by the enemy the next day. Where trench warfare did make a difference was in the loss of life. Each inconsequential exchange of land resulted in high casualties. In early 1916 the Germans attempted to break through the French lines with a massive, concentrated attack at Verdun. After ten months of continuous carnage, the Battle of Ver-

OOPS

As World War I settled into a war of attrition, Germany's greatest fear was that the United States would enter the war on the side of the Allies. When President Wilson demanded that Germany cease unrestricted submarine warfare in 1916, rather than risk the wrath of the U.S., Germany agreed. But German Foreign Minister Arthur Zimmerman believed that sooner or later, the U.S. would weigh in against Germany. To provide for this eventuality, in 1917 he dashed off a telegram to the President of Mexico, proposing a German-Mexican-Japanese alliance should the U.S. declare war against Germany. In return for its support, Mexico would regain Texas, New Mexico, and Arizona from the defeated U.S.

Zimmerman's telegram was read with glee by British intelligence, who had intercepted and broken the coded message. They promptly posted the text to President Wilson, who had it published in the American press. When Wilson asked Congress for a declaration of war in April of that year, public outrage over Zimmerman's proposal helped decide the issue.

The Western Front
- – – – Furthest German advance 1914
- ·········· Furthest German advance 1918
- ——— Trench Warfare 1914-1917
- —·— Armistice line 11 Nov 1918

dun ended without resolution. The battle had no strategic impact. The only way you could tell the difference between its start in February and its finish in December was the fact that there were a million fewer soldiers around to fight in December. Here's the dreadful tally:

Nation	Losses (Dead, Missing, Wounded)
Great Britain	400,000
France	200,000
Germany	500,000

That works out to about 153 either dead, wounded, or missing every hour of every day, over a period of 300 days. Never was human brutality so efficiently executed.

In January of 1917 the Germans once again tried to break the deadlock—this time, through the use of submarines. German leaders calculated that, if submarines could cut off all shipping to and from Great Britain, Germany could starve the British out of the war in six months. It was a calculated risk. In 1915 a German submarine had sunk the *Lusitania,* an English passenger ship, believing it to be carrying arms. A number of Americans had been on the *Lusitania,* and

The news that a German submarine had torpedoed the Lusitania, killing over a thousand passengers (with 128 US citizens among them), outraged Americans, contributing to public support for the United States' entry into the war.

American protests had forced the Germans to discontinue submarine attacks on passenger vessels. Now, by resuming unrestricted submarine warfare, the Germans were betting they could finish off Great Britain before the United States could make a difference. On April 2, 1917, President Woodrow Wilson, in an address to the joint houses of Congress, called for a declaration of war in protest of the German resumption of the use of submarines. He got it.

If Germany was disturbed by the United States entering the war, within six months they had reason to rejoice when the Russians made their exit.

RUSSIAN REVOLUTION VER. 1.0

In 1917 the Russians produced two revolutions, the February Revolution and the October Revolution, so called because they took place in March and November. (The Russians went by the Julian calendar until 1918. At least they didn't follow the example of the French Revolution, or we might have ended up with another Thermidor on our hands.)

In 1914, when the war came, it provided Czar Nicholas II with a temporary respite from the internal discord that had been steadily growing. Nicholas led his country into the conflict with near unanimous support; but the war served only to point out Russia's internal weakness (much as the Crimean War had done in the last century, during Alexander I's reign). Still comparatively backward economically and industrially, Russia was unable to sustain a long campaign.

The home front began to suffer as troops continued to siphon off needed goods. Then, as arms and supplies dwindled, Russian armies suffered a series of military defeats at the hands of well-equipped German forces.

Despite striking workers, revolutionary agitators, and warnings from the always irritating Duma, Nicho-

---

TODAY HE'D HAVE HIS OWN INFOMERCIAL

The "Mad Monk" of Russia wasn't an old-time professional wrestler, but a New Age professional quack. Grigory Rasputin (1872–1916) managed to attach himself to Czarina Alexandra with promises that he could heal her son's hemophilia. Having won her confidence, he managed to get some of his buddies appointed to office, and soon the palace was filled with faith-healing charlatans giving new meaning to the word "debauched." Rasputin's influence was so great that when Nicholas II decided, in 1915, to drop by the front and see how the war was going, Rasputin ended up pretty much in charge of the country.

Despite his position, Rasputin was not a very popular guy. He aroused popular resentment with his imperious, amoral behavior, and alienated the aristocracy as an uneducated commoner who had cast an unholy spell over the czarina. In December 1916 a group of czarists threw him a theme party. The theme: kill Rasputin. They tried poisoning him, but he didn't seem to mind. Then they shot him, but he survived that. Finally they threw him in the Neva River. Drowning—*that* he minded.

las refused to consider any action that might under-
mine his authority. He dissolved the Duma and
ordered the army to disperse striking workers in the
capital, St. Petersburg. The army, however, found it
had more in common with the workers than with the
czar, and ended up joining the general strike in
March 1917. Nicholas, isolated without the support of
the armed forces, abdicated. The Duma reassembled
and drafted the Provisional Government.

RUSSIAN REVOLUTION, VER. 1.1

The Provisional Government made some popular
moves—getting rid of many of the czar's restrictions
on religious and intellectual freedom, for example—
but it could never manage to become the dominant
political force. Real power remained with the soviets
(councils) previously established by socialist workers
to organize against the czarist regime. The Duma may
have had legal authority, but the Petrograd Soviet
(this primary soviet was based in the renamed capital
of Petrograd) had an impressive veto: the armed
forces.

The instability of the situation made Russia a kind
of Revolutionary Lottery, as exiles like Lenin, Stalin,
and Leon Trotsky (Lenin's second in command was
in New York City at the time of the February Revolution) came running home to take their chances. Soon
various factions were competing for power. Bolsheviks,
Mensheviks, Moderates, Liberals. The Bolsheviks, with
Lenin in command, dissolved the Provisional Govern-

*Tsar Nicholas II and the Tsarina Alexandra:
the last Romanov rulers.*

WHAT GOES AROUND, COMES AROUND

What do the following cities have in common?:

> *St. Petersburg:* Founded by Czar Peter the Great in 1703, it became the Russian capital in 1713.

> *Petrograd:* Named by Nicholas II in 1914.

> *Leningrad:* Created in 1924 to honor Lenin.

All the same city. Today it goes by the name of . . . St. Petersburg.

ment on November 17, 1917. The new Soviet regime discontinued fighting in December 1917; Lenin believed the war a waste of time, since the revolution would spread throughout Europe soon enough, destroying all political institutions and boundaries. In March 1918 the communists signed the Treaty of Brest-Litovsk, which enabled Germany to concentrate its total war effort on the western front. In July the Soviet government wrapped up its housecleaning by executing Nicholas II and his family—a cruel act which ended centuries of czarist rule and won Ingrid Bergman an Academy Award as *Anastasia*.

WORLD WAR 1, GERMANY 0

The Germans, freed from the eastern front, roared into March 1918 like a lion. Amassing 6,000 guns on a front of some fifty miles, laying down first an artillery barrage, then a gas attack, they began the "Great March Offensive." After initial success, the Germans met with tremendous resistance bolstered by the presence of the American Expeditionary Force, which after a year of equipping and training began to play a major part in the war. In the second Battle of the Marne (July–August 1918), American forces withstood the German and then counterattacked.

The "Really Rapid March Backwards" now began as the German High Command saw its exhausted and disheartened troops pushed back by Allied forces. Meanwhile, Kaiser William II decided that going down with the ship of state was unbecoming for an em-

**YOU CAN'T TELL THE PLAYERS
WITHOUT A PROGRAM**

Herewith, the major combatants in World War I:

For the *Central Powers* (named for the central location of Germany and Austria-Hungary): Germany, Austria-Hungry, and Turkey, in 1914; joined by Bulgaria in 1915.

For the *Allied Forces:* Serbia, Russia, Great Britain, France, all in 1914; joined by Montenegro (1914), Italy (1915), Romania (1916), the United States (1917), and Greece (1918).

peror—so he abdicated and went into exile in the Netherlands to write his memoirs. Germany declared itself a republic. Fearful of a complete military collapse, the High Command urged the new German government to seek peace along the lines proposed by President Woodrow Wilson. The German government did, and the fighting ceased at 11:00 A.M. on November 11, 1918. Thousands of Londoners and Parisians took to the streets, rejoicing at the war's end.

And then the bill came.

THE TOLL

The "fresh and joyous war" that Germany had anticipated, that glorious opportunity for heroism anticipated by British youth, had gone on for four cruel years. Encouraged by economic competition, it ruined whole nations. In 1918 the cost of the war had risen to approximately $1,163,000 per minute. Assisted by an imperial search for territory, it produced huge tracts of desolation. Driven by nationalist pride, its waste of life was horrendous. In France, the country that endured the most casualties, one-half of the male population in its twenties never lived to become thirty-something. The loss of so many soldiers produced statistics that could only be given poignant meaning by reducing them to one single figure: Every country erected a monument to an unknown soldier.

Statistics can only hint at the deep, collective, psychological damage done to a world astounded at its capacity for senseless slaughter. "The war has ruined us for everything," says one of the characters in Erich Remarque's *All Quiet on the Western Front*. The "lost generation," those young men who had fought, returned home, and could not find themselves, now wandered aimlessly about—fictional characters like Jay

MOW 'EM DOWN, STITCH 'EM UP

The two most popular mass-produced industrial machines during World War I were the sewing machine and the machine gun. The sewing machine stitched up; the machine gun cut down. The sewing machine made uniforms with which to clothe the soldiers; the machine gun made corpses out of the uniformed men. Each machine repeated its action quickly and regularly. Each machine achieved its results by a piercing action. Together, these two machines expressed the moral ambivalence attached to industrialization, the help and harm it so easily produced.

Gatsby and real-life ones like Adolf Hitler. Statesmen shook their heads in dismay, comforted only by the costly knowledge that never again would man resort to such awful horror. The Great War was, in the words of Woodrow Wilson, the "war to end all wars." He never lived to see the sequel.

WHO'S GOING TO PAY FOR THIS MESS?

With the armistice signed, it was once again time for the obligatory "pick-up-the-pieces" party. The victors assembled in Paris to work out postwar Europe. As at the Congress of Vienna, there were four big winners calling the shots, this time including Great Britain, France, Italy, and the United States. *Italy?* Wasn't it part of the Triple Alliance, along with Germany and Austria-Hungary? It was, but once war broke out the Italians decided not to play—until the Allies convinced them to come in against their old oppressor, Austria.

To the victorious nations, the surest way to keep peace was to put a lid on Germany. The Versailles Treaty established a buffer zone between Germany and France in the Rhineland and transferred territory from Germany to France, Poland, and the new state of Czechoslovakia. It reduced the German army to a maximum of 100,000 and forbid Germany to manufacture military aircraft and tanks. The killer section of the treaty—Article 231, the so-called "war guilt" clause—declared that Germany had to accept the en-

German submarines being dismantled after WWI. The rest of the fleet had already been scuttled by the Germans themselves, in order to prevent the ships from becoming property of the Allies.

tire blame for the war. This meant that Germany was saddled with the payment of "reparations," a diplomatic nicety that comes down to "You broke it, you bought it." It was going to be an expensive peace for the Germans, considering that so much of the Continent had been trashed.

The Germans might have claimed that the Austrian Empire had started it all by attacking Serbia, but the two states that had precipitated the war no longer existed. The last Hapsburg emperor, Charles I, could only watch as Hungary and Czechoslovakia broke away in 1918. Finally, Austria itself became a republic, ending over 500 years of Hapsburg rule. That same year Serbia, Croatia, and Montenegro had joined to become the Kingdom of Serbs, Croats, and Slovenes— an accurate but unwieldy name which eventually gave way, in 1929, to Yugoslavia.

BELEAGUERED NATIONS

President Wilson came to Paris prepared to play a twentieth-century Metternich. Peace wasn't enough for Wilson; he wanted to ensure future harmony as well. To that end, he persuaded Europe to accept an agency of international government that would peacefully regulate issues of potential conflict. Called the League of Nations, it was designed to function as an international parliament. Officially founded in 1920 with its headquarters in Geneva, it never had a chance.

For one thing, the United States never even joined, which was somewhat embarrassing to the man who had thought it up. And although it featured elaborately devised mechanisms to settle disputes, it had no real tools to enforce its decisions. Its chief weapon was the use of economic sanctions—a boycott on trade with the offending nation. Even that rarely worked. After Italy invaded Ethiopia in 1935, the League ordered a boycott against the aggressor. It made no difference. Great Britain and France were reluctant to impose League-ordered sanctions that might lead to armed conflict with Italy. International protest against the invasion of Ethiopia amounted to little more than

JUST WRITE YOUR FIRST NAME, MIDDLE NAME, LAST NAME, NICKNAME, ALIAS, MONIKER . . .

War generates more than trench mouth. War produces nicknames and legends. Here are a few:

T. E. Lawrence, (1888–1935) or "Lawrence of Arabia": Led a unified Arab force against the Turks in World War I.

Manfred von Richtofen (1892–1918), or "the Red Baron": Shot down at the old age (for pilots) of 26, after having downed more than seventy enemy aircraft.

Gertrude Margarete Zelle (1876–1917), or "Mata Hari": Spied for the Germans, then died at the hands of the French.

Erwin Rommel (1891–1944), or "the Desert Fox": Commanded the feared *Afrika Korps* for Hitler. Accused of complicity in a plot on the Führer's life, he committed suicide.

Josef Dzhugashvili (1879–1953), or "Josef Stalin" Preferred a surname that meant "man of steel" over one that meant "dzhugashvili."

Josip Broz (1892–1980), or "Tito": Served as the president of Post-WWII Yugoslavia.

**JUST WRITE YOUR FIRST NAME,
MIDDLE NAME, LAST NAME, NICKNAME,
ALIAS, MONIKER . . . (*continued*)**

Saxe-Coburg-Gotha, or "Windsor": The name of Great Britain's royal family after 1917, when German names fell out of favor. The German name came from the fact that Queen Victoria had married the German Prince Albert. (Elizabeth II's children are known as Mountbatten-Windsor, reflecting her marriage to Philip Mountbatten, whose own surname had once been Battenberg.)

noise, since Italy continued to get its most needed war resource—oil—through trade.

As far as membership was concerned, the League of Nations was less like a European Tribunal than a European Health Spa. Countries came when they felt like it, quit when they wanted, and ignored the League's suggestions when they pleased. Germany was excluded until 1926, then quit in 1933 when Hitler gained power. The Soviet Union was admitted only in 1926, while Japan left in 1931, as did Italy in 1935. The two major democratic powers, Great Britain and France, were never enthusiastic about the League. No one mourned its passing as the 1930s ended. By then, there was a better reason to start mourning—the peace of Paris was turning out to be merely an intermission.

THE POSTWAR . . . MAKE THAT THE INTERWAR ERA

Over here, it was called the Roaring Twenties. Over there, it was known as the "crazy years." Either way, the 1920s was a decade of relieved distraction—"going to hell gaily," as one English editorial writer described it. The Great War, it seemed, hadn't just leveled a generation; it had severed all ties to the past. The sense of liberation was almost palpable. Traditional forms, mores, and credos were either dead or irrelevant—the war had seen to that. Now the only thing to do was look to the future.

The sudden freedom—not just from war but also from constraint—made Europe a place of cultural excitement. Americans were drawn to it to express their literary and artistic talents. It was the setting of the novels of Ernest Hemingway and F. Scott Fitzgerald, of George Gershwin's orchestral piece, *An American in Paris,* and of exported blues and jazz music, played and celebrated by African Americans. It was the Europe of the Berlin cabaret and the Parisian *Folies Bergère;* of long-hooded, hand-crafted Bugatti automobiles. It was the Europe that encouraged art deco (named after the International Exposition of Decorative Arts, held in Paris in 1925), a style consummated in New York City's Chrysler Building. It was the Europe of the sleek, functional architecture of the *Bauhaus,* the Weimar workshop that fostered the "international style," and produced the kind of glass-sheathed, cereal-box-shaped buildings now found in every major city. It was the Europe of Picasso's cubism and Salvador Dali's surrealism: the one celebrating three-dimensionality; the other, the space and time of dream and fantasy. It was the Europe of the English detective novel, such as Agatha Christie's *Murder on the Orient Express;* and the German psychological film, such as *The Cabinet of Dr. Caligari.* It was the Europe of Chanel perfume, Lalique crystal, and Rolex watches. It was a Europe of exceptional elegance and artistic experimentation.

The only problem was that all this lovely elegance was built on a precarious economy riddled and fissured by the war. The once capital-rich nations of France and Great Britain were now debtor nations, their accumulated gold resting in the vaults of Fort Knox—repayment of huge loans by the American government to finance the production of armaments by American manufacturers. Their plight was hardly helped by the entrance of war veterans into the workforce. The British General Strike of 1926, hard on the heels of a coal strike, brought out nearly 2.5 million of the 6 million union workers in the British Isles. The severe German inflation of 1923, caused by war reparations, wiped out family savings and much of Germany's hope for a better life under democracy.

A PUNISHING PEACE

In drafting the Versailles Treaty, one of the Allies' greatest concerns was that even in defeat, Germany was still potentially the most powerful nation in Europe. The Ruhr Valley, heart of Germany's industrial might, could

THE PROVING GROUND TO END ALL PROVING GROUNDS

In terms of weapons technology, the First World War was nothing more than a rough draft, a laboratory in which to field test new weapons of destruction. Deadly inventions that showed real promise would become staples of the next war; destructive lemons were discontinued. Here are some of both:

Tank—Although the idea of armored transport dates back to the armadillo, it wasn't until 1916 that the British combined an internal combustion engine, rotating track (instead of wheels), and a few guns to produce a viable offensive weapon. A year later, in the French town of Cambrai, the British broke through German lines using these new tanks. By the time World War II began, the Germans had made the tank one of the building blocks of its army.

Zeppelin—1916 also saw the first bombing "run" by a Zeppelin attacking Paris, but the drawbacks with these airships soon became apparent: traveling at a snail-like 20 miles per hour, the flying whales became sitting ducks to enemy airplanes. In World War II they were used primarily as scouting vehicles.

Depth Charge—Necessity was the mother of this timely invention. With German U-boots wreaking havoc on Allied ships during the First World War, a method of disabling the submerged ships was needed. The depth charge made use of the fact that it wasn't necessary for an explosive to make contact with a submarine to cause damage—an underwater explosion would create a shock wave that could cripple a nearby submarine.

**THE PROVING GROUND TO END ALL
PROVING GROUNDS (*continued*)** . . . .

Chemical Warfare—"Mustard Gas" was the most
terrifying of chemical agents introduced by the Germans during WWI. Its use was discontinued by international agreement after the war, less for its horrific
effects than for its susceptibility to slight changes in
wind.

---

all too quickly restore its Continental dominance. This
was not a comforting thought to European peacemak-
ers, who clamped down hard on Germany—politically,
economically, and psychologically.

Keeping the boot on the German nation's neck (a
French phrase of the time) only generated German
resentment against the "dictated peace" *(Diktat),* and
troubled the new Weimar Republic—so named because its constitution had been drawn up in the city
of Weimar, the hometown of Germany's greatest poet,
Johann Wolfgang von Goethe. The republic, formed
by a coalition of social democrats in 1918 after Kaiser
William's abdication, was in trouble from its inception,
since its leaders had signed the punitive Versailles
Treaty. The severe peace and the precariousness of
the Germany economy chipped away at the legitimacy
of the democratic republic. Reparations quickly de-
pleted German gold reserves, then began to eat up
goods as the Germans were forced to turn over assets
to the Allied repo men. As ocean liners, railroad engines, airships, and Marlene Dietrich went to the victo-

rious powers, the German economy took a nose dive.

Scavenging amid the political and economy debris of postwar Germany was a rowdy, uniformed and uninformed group of hecklers and thugs calling themselves the National Socialist German Workers Party (or "Nazi," from *nationalsozialistiche*), headed by Adolf Hitler. In the 1920s the Nazis were hardly a major political force; they were a public nuisance, not a national threat. But their platform was already well established, designed to play to the general discontent: repudiate the Versailles Treaty, unseat the "November Traitors" who had signed it, and revive the economy by re-arming the nation. It was an attractive alternative to the Weimar Republic's democratic haplessness.

DISORDER

Winston Churchill, who as England's prime minister would lead that country through World War II, once claimed that democracy was the worst form of government—except for all the others. Churchill's remark came just after Germany, Austria, and Czechoslovakia became democratic republics in 1918—seeming proof that the world had been made safe for democracy. Unfortunately, this initial bright burst of democratic principle was short-lived. In just one decade, democracy seemed an inept and indecisive means of government, good for little more than generating domestic strife. Confronted with unemployment, depreciated currency, and aging industries, the democracies of Europe reeled into the 1930s.

Conditions seemed to demand some sort of quick, decisive action, but Europe's democratic nations were barely able to rule on a day-to-day basis. Bold action was beyond their reach. The byword of the time wasn't decision but compromise. Only Great Britain, among the leading democratic nations, had a two-party system. The others had several parties that vied for leadership and that, by their very number, frequently required compromise in order to assure a coalition. Weimar Germany even introduced proportional representation, which assured that every party that gained a sufficient number of votes would have seats in the legislative body. Neither plurality nor majority was necessary. The result came to be known as "splinter politics." Political kindling is more like it.

Then the latest American export arrived on the Continent—economic depression. It had begun with the famous crash of the American stock market on October 29, 1929, and brought both massive unemployment and a widespread sense of despair. Wobbly European democracies were now faced with demands that the government respond as a social system for the well-being of the populace. Popular front governments, consisting of coalitions of centrist and leftist parties, attempted to find solutions. The most famous was the Popular Front in France (1936–1937), in which the new premier, Leon Blum, introduced paid vacations, nationalized industries, and the forty-hour workweek.

On top of all this, the colonies were now starting to act up. Nationalist movements in colonized territories inspired resistance to imperialism, spreading the word through newspapers and strikes. Close to the seat of the British Empire, the Irish gained independence in 1921 as the Irish Free State, taking control of the island, excepting only Protestant Ulster in the north. In India, Mohandas Gandhi (1869–1948), perhaps the most popular of the resistance leaders, used the technique of passive resistance to embarrass and dislodge the English. His most notable weapon was the hunger strike. ("I'm not hungry; I'll just picket.") In northern Africa, an armed uprising of nomads forced the Spanish out of their part of Morocco, then swept into French Morocco at great military and financial cost to France. Everywhere in the colonial world, unrest forced either violent repression or reform. Imperialism no longer seemed quite so righteous. Moral opinion was swinging to the nationalist colonies, as many critics began to question the value of continuing the colonial enterprise.

Even in the countries where democracy survived, home-grown fascism proved an incessant irritant. The British Fascist Union turned out to be merely a cranky lot; Austrian fascism, on the other hand, was sponsored by Chancellor Engelbert Dollfuss (1892–1934) and resulted in a brief civil war between February 12 and 15, 1934. The Austrian fascists defeated socialist forces and abolished all parties except for Dollfuss's own—including the Austrian Nazi Party. The chancellor thought he had established an independent fascist republic that would be Germany's equal. He was wrong. A few months later Dollfuss was assassinated by the Nazis; four years later Austria would be annexed by Germany.

HITLER HITS THE HEIGHTS

The Weimar Republic is remembered best for its good intentions, which only helped pave Germany's eventual road to hell. Contempt for the republic's ineffectuality was shared by Nazis, Communists, Socialists, even the occasional loon who advocated some sort of kaiser role in government. In 1923 Hitler backed up his contempt with an attempted coup against the Weimar Republic. The Munich *Putsch* failed; Hitler was sent to prison, where he wrote his autobiography, *Mein Kampf (My Struggle)*. *Mein Kampf* was, appropriately enough, the antithesis of Diderot's *Encylopédie*, published almost two centuries previously: Although everyone in Germany eventually owned a copy, no one seems to have actually read it.

After being released from prison in 1924 (eight months for trying to overthrow the government?), he set about rebuilding the Nazi Party—this time by attracting votes. With the Weimar Republic unable to forge any sort of stable ruling coalition, and the country weakened by depression and unemployment, the Nazi Party's membership increased dramatically. In 1932 the Nazis were the largest party represented in the *Reichstag*. They did not, however, command a majority of seats. Any effective government would have to be a coalition between two of three parties: the Social Democrats, the Communists, and the Nazis. Hitler's manipulations blocked every attempt to form a government. President Paul von Hindenburg (1847–1934)—whose brilliant military career spanned the Seven Weeks' War, the Franco-Prussian War, and

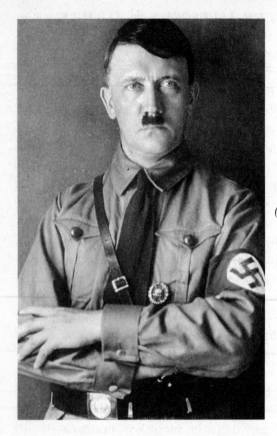

Adolf Hitler (1889–1945): Corporal, Chancellor, Dictator.

World War I—tried to put an end to the gridlock by appointing Hitler chancellor. What he inadvertently put an end to was the Weimar Republic.

When Hitler took office on January 30, 1933, Germany didn't just get a new chancellor; they got a Nazi Party organized to take over. A fire that destroyed the *Reichstag* (how convenient!) gave the Nazis arson as an excuse for violent suppression of the Communists;

with the left wing out of the picture, Hitler now controlled the *Reichstag*. Before the year was out, the *Reichstag* had made the Nazis the only legal political party in Germany. Hitler, as absolute master of the party, had legal authority over every living being in Germany. Without ever having won a popular election, Adolf Hitler had become the law. He thus joined Benito Mussolini, appointed premier of Italy in 1922, and Josef Stalin, who by 1929 had taken complete control of the Soviet Union, as the head of a totalitarian European nation.

FOLLOW THE LEADER

One of the few original things Benito Mussolini ever did was coin the word *totalitarianism*. It describes the dictatorships of Italy, Germany, and the Soviet Union—specifically, those states' attempts to exercise total control over all aspects of society. Complete control was never quite achieved, but it wasn't for want of trying. Opposition was severely repressed and all too often simply exterminated. Whether fascist or communist, these regimes turned Enlightenment tradition on its head by exalting the collective over the individual. Self-realization, personal dissent, compromise, individual liberty and value disappeared in the ascendancy of the group—whether it be nation, party, or soviet.

Where democracy seemed to offer nothing but indecision, totalitarian systems were capable of bold, decisive, confident action. The Nazis promised a swift

Il Duce (Leader), Benito Mussolini, fascist dictator of Italy.

end to Germany's economic depression and national humiliation; Italian Fascists guaranteed an end to Italy's unemployment and the resulting threat of socialist revolution; Soviet Communists trumpeted the end of class and national distinctions. All three demanded just one thing in return: complete surrender of personal liberty to the party. For many it seemed a small price to pay.

The party controlled the media and generated propaganda ("the party line"), determined education curriculum, and imposed state planning of the economy. The continued supremacy of the single party was reinforced through use of the plebiscite—a general election on one specific issue, such as: "Now that I already have complete power, and will punish anyone with the nerve to dissent, would you like to vote for me?" The plebiscite was, for the most part, an international public relations ploy designed to give totalitarian governments a veneer of legitimacy.

Each of these systems was a perversion of the pastoral idyll of shepherd and flock, patriarch and family, each with its version of the infallible leader (*führer* and

Italian workers in Berlin demonstrate their solidarity with the Germans. When Nazi Germany and fascist Italy concluded a 1936 alliance, it was said that all Europe now revolved around the Rome-Berlin "axis," giving rise to the term "Axis Powers."

duce both mean leader) directing the destinies of its people. The relationship between leader and nation was half political, half religious. Surrounded by trappings of costume and ceremony, the leader was seen as a charismatic, spiritually endowed being, whose special gifts and power distinguished him from all others. This was the cult of personality.

This cult's specialty was the mass rally, at which the leader would stand elevated on a dias or balcony, high above the crowds gathered before him. A German social critic claimed that Nazi Party rallies, with their thousands of flags and tens of thousands of participants, had made politics a popular art form. Its popularity extended to Italy, where Mussolini waved his

In 1938 the city of Nuremberg hosted the Nazis' greatest celebration. Seven years later it would play host to the war crimes trials of Nazi leaders.

hands and pounded his chest during open-air speeches before the thousands gathered under the balcony of his office in Rome. The spectacle reached Moscow's Red Square, where the Communist Party leadership assembled atop Lenin's mausoleum to view the annual May Day military parade. As columns of soldiers marched past and bright banners unfurled, party officials kept one wary eye on the man who had replaced Lenin. More than a few wished that it was Josef Stalin who was buried in Lenin's tomb.

MAN OF STEEL

Josef Stalin (his adopted name means "man of steel") built his own particular cult of personality in two ways: by dragging the Soviet Union into the modern industrial age and by eliminating anyone who didn't think he should have a cult of personality. Brusque and pragmatic, a shrewd administrator and political manipulator, Stalin spent his time as the Communist general secretary under Lenin learning the ins and outs of the party machine. After Lenin's death in 1924, Stalin bested his political rivals in a four-year struggle to assume control of the party—managing to have his old friend and closest political rival, Leon Trotsky, expelled from the party and eventually banished from the Soviet Union. (In 1940 Trotsky would be assassinated in Mexico by a Stalinist agent.)

Having consolidated power, Stalin began a crash

program of industrialization designed to transform the Soviet Union from a backward agricultural state into a modern European power. The brutal pace he set for the country was matched only by the brutality with which he enforced his plans. He dispossessed an entire class of people—the *kulaks,* a group of over 5 million peasant farm owners—and placed their land under State control. Using the agricultural harvest as seed money for building industry, he helped create homegrown famine. As the country staggered under the hardship of Stalin's breakneck pace, voices of protest came from a starving, exhausted population, as well as from Stalin's political opponents.

They were cruelly silenced. In 1934 Stalin began what is known as the Great Purge, in which he methodically exterminated every real and imagined enemy he could find. Political opponents, suspected counter-revolutionaries, friends, family, members of the military, policemen, intellectuals, and artists were summarily tried and executed. Others simply vanished at the hands of the secret police. Millions disappeared into a system of prisons so widespread that one of those who survived, Aleksandr Solzhenitsyn (b. 1918), referred to it as *the Gulag Archipelago,* in his book by the same name (GULAG being the acronym for the camps' administrative body). Siberia acquired its reputation as the labor-camp capital of the world.

By 1939 the Soviet Union had become a juggernaut of industrial might and political terror under Stalin's personal direction—a machine that, by the end of his twenty-four-year reign, would sacrifice over *20 million* people to the totalitarian order. The same number of Russians would die preserving that order in the coming war.

ORDER

Benito Mussolini once boasted that he had made the trains run on time. The phrase today has a chilling effect, for it represents the ruthlessness of totalitarian states that, in their glorification of order, imposed conformity and exterminated unwanted elements with all the sensitivity of a steamroller. Huge, heavy-handed, and rigid bureaucracies promulgated regulations for every aspect of human activity. The Nazi party not only determined where, when, and how Germans were allowed to work, but regulated where, when, and how they could *play* as well—by controlling Germany's recreational organizations under a Nazi program called *Kraft durch Freude* ("strength through joy"). In Italy, the government went so far as to decree that shaking hands was officially out, substituting an old Roman salute in its place.

The state was redesigned to resemble a huge machine, every part in its place. This was the heyday of efficiency, its desirability elaborated by Frederick W. Taylor, an American engineer. His book, *Scientific Management* (1886), led to the first major time-motion studies, by which human behavior could be adapted to the needs of the machine. "Taylorization" was widely accepted in Europe and equally criticized. Lenin praised it; Aldous Huxley ridiculed it in *Brave New World* (1932). In Huxley's novel about a future time

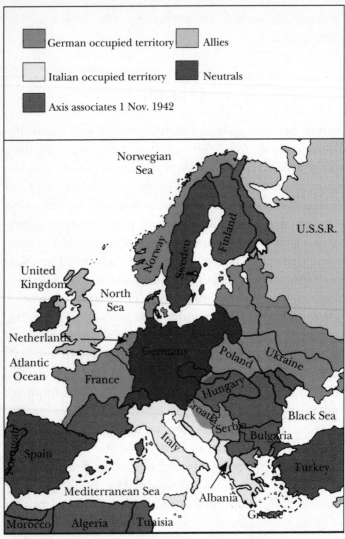

German occupied territory

Italian occupied territory

Axis associates 1 Nov. 1942

Allies

Neutrals

Norwegian
Sea

U.S.S.R.

Norway

Sweden

Finland

United
Kingdom

North
Sea

Netherlands

Atlantic
Ocean

Germany

Poland

Ukraine

France

Hungary

Croatia

Serbia

Black Sea

Bulgaria

Spain

Italy

Turkey

Mediterranean Sea

Albania

Greece

Morocco

Algeria

Tunisia

*By 1942, fascism, once only one of Europe's many
political movements, was threatening to become Europe's
only political movements.*

of order and efficiency, defined as the sixth century A. F. ("after Ford"), test-tube babies are divided into three classes, each endowed with the necessary intelligence to do its assigned functions in blissful innocence and without doubt of its status.

Huxley's ridicule was closer to the truth than anyone cared to admit. If the state was a machine, its citizens were simply parts. Parts that worked smoothly and quietly were oiled. Those that made noise were removed and discarded.

Dissent was eliminated and obedience ensured through organized, legal terror. The totalitarian regime was a police state, in which secret police (the Gestapo in Nazi Germany was the most notorious of the lot, but the Italian and Soviet counterparts known as OVRA and OGPU were just as effective) seized "enemies of the state" and carried them to imprisonment or execution. One of the most ruthless and sadly remembered acts of officially sanctioned brutality was *Kristallnacht* ("Night of Crystal")—November 9, 1938, when the Nazis organized a night of "spontaneous" popular rioting against synagogues and Jewish-owned stores throughout Germany, beating any who dared protest. It was but an omen of things to come.

WARS D'OEUVRES

Once Europe's fascist states had consolidated power at home, they turned outward. Confident, belligerent, and hungry, loudly proclaiming their moral righteousness and territorial destiny, they tested democracy's resolve—and found it sorely lacking. Democratic nations, racked by depression, hampered by the inefficiency of their political systems, and committed to avoiding another war, reacted to fascist expansion with nothing more than words.

In 1935 Benito Mussolini sought to construct a "Third Rome," a new Roman Empire, by invading Ethiopia despite general European opposition. This blatant act of aggression was justified by the usual contention—border disputes between Ethiopia and Italian Eritrea. The war went on for more than a year, as the Ethiopians offered stiff resistance. The Ethiopian emperor, Haile Selassie, pleaded for assistance from the League of Nations, as well as from individual European powers. His pleas reached sympathetic ears; Italian aggression was roundly condemned and sanctions were officially imposed. The only hitch was that the Italians didn't particularly care; they continued the war until they got what they wanted anyway. Italy's newest colony was the last to be established in Africa and lasted just about four years. It would be quickly overrun by the English in World War II.

More significant to the Continent itself was the Spanish Civil War (1936–1939)—often referred to as the "novelists' war" because of the participation of authors Ernest Hemingway, André Malraux, and George Orwell. The Loyalists, soldiers and citizens supporting the established republic in Spain, fought the Rebels, a fascist-inspired military revolt led by Francisco Franco, a general just previously stationed in the Canary Islands. The war was brutal and long, concluding only months before World War II began.

Both Hitler and Mussolini supplied aid, troops, and equipment to Franco. The Soviet Union, strengthened by industrialization, sought to stem the tide of international fascism by supporting the Loyalists. Many volunteers from around the Western world arrived to support the Loyalists, including the "Abraham Lincoln Brigade," a contingent of Americans.

Franco won, celebrating his victory with a vindictive wave of arrest, imprisonment, and execution for anyone who had dared oppose him. Spain would endure his repressive rule for nearly forty years. (He died in 1975—and remains dead to this day.) Hitler's reign would be much shorter, but much more appalling. For the next five years, Hitler conducted his horrific light-and-sound show, a hell-on-earth that destroyed land and person, home and hope. "Hitler is a monster of wickedness," exclaimed Winston Churchill in a speech of 1941. For once, the prime minister had understated his case.

HITLER AND APPEASEMENT

Hitler believed in little other than his destiny, which he considered inextricably bound with that of Germany. So sure was he of himself that he was the first world leader to fly regularly in then still-primitive aircraft. He believed it was his holy mission to restore Germany to the position that befit its moral and racial superiority. His Third Reich, he claimed, would last a thousand years. (*Reich* is simply German for empire. Hitler numbered the Holy Roman Empire as Germany's first Reich; Bismarck's was the second.) His self-assurance was boosted by a series of diplomatic successes as he tested the resolve of the other European powers. And with each failure of that resolve, the aura of Hitler's invincibility grew.

As he began his "restoration" of the German empire, Hitler knew that Germany was in a precarious position. If one of his belligerent moves resulted in a show of force against Germany, his Third Reich would simply collapse. He feared confrontation. What he consistently got was appeasement.

The thought of another war was simply too abhorrent to both Great Britain and France; neither wished to repeat what they had endured during World War I. The French foreign minister, Aristide Briand, had argued in the 1920s for "peace at any price." A "Peace Ballot," initiated in Great Britain in 1935, resulted in 11 million votes for reduction of armaments by international agreement.

In this atmosphere, some political analysts believed (or perhaps wanted to believe) that Hitler merely wanted to incorporate German-speaking populations into his Third Reich. Others saw Hitler as a bulwark against Communist Russia. Still others thought that he was so strong as to be nearly irresistible. Whatever the rationale, the policy worked out to the same thing: whine a little, but give Hitler what he wants and everyone can sleep at night, knowing that war has been avoided.

That attitude enabled Hitler to re-arm Germany, take back the Rhineland, and annex Austria with both ease and speed. The culmination of the policy of appeasement was the Munich Agreement of September 1938, when the leaders of Great Britain and France sat down with those of Nazi Germany and Fascist Italy. Their purpose: to decide the fate of the Republic of Czechoslovakia. One portion of that republic, the Sudetenland, was home to a large German population. Hitler had demanded that this territory be joined to his Third Reich—or else. Fearing the else, without consulting representatives from the Czechs, France and Great Britain acquiesced to Hitler's demands. British Prime Minister Neville Chamberlain (1869–1940) returned to cheering London crowds, announcing proudly that the Munich Agreement had achieved "peace in our time."

Hitler, triumphant and sure of himself, took not just the Sudetenland but the rest of Czechoslovakia as well, in March 1939.

Poland was next on his list. Though both France and Great Britain now vowed to support Poland if Hitler should make a move there, he was more concerned with the Soviet Union response. The Western European powers had repeatedly demonstrated a lack of resolve in the face of German demands. But the Soviet Union might well take offense at a German invasion of Poland, which would place German troops within marching distance of Moscow. On August 23, 1939, Germany announced the signing of a nonaggression pact with the Soviet Union, agreeing to preserve peace between them. The deal-maker was a secret clause by which the two powers agreed to split Poland between them. Hitler lost little time claiming his half.

ANOTHER WORLD WAR

Hitler's duplicity in Czechoslovakia had finally convinced France and Great Britain of his true motives. When he began making belligerent noises toward Poland they called his bluff. There would be no second Munich. If Hitler wanted Poland, he would have to take it by force. On September 1, 1939, that's exactly what he did.

The Nazi war machine rolled swiftly into Poland in a relentless surge of annihilation and annexation. This was *blitzkrieg*—lighting warfare—in which dive-bombers and tanks supported fast-moving infantry. Loudspeakers in Warsaw played Chopin's famous piece, *Marche militaire,* to inspire the population. But the Germans were coming with tanks and bombers; the Polish had only cavalry to resist. Poland was defeated within a month, but not before Great Britain and France had reluctantly declared war, two days after the German invasion began. Neville Chamberlain, the Conservative prime minister of Great Britain, and Édouard Daladier, the centrist premier of France, had done all they could to avoid war. How could they have known Hitler's true intentions?

For one, they might have taken the time to read *Mein Kampf.* It was all right there.

NEW AND IMPROVED!

Sequels tend to mimic the original while adding a little extra something of their own; World War II was no different. Like its predecessor, it centered on a powerful and aggressive Germany opposed by an alliance of France and Great Britain (and eventually joined by Russia). Like its predecessor, it witnessed the late entry of the United States. Like its predecessor, it had a western and an eastern front. Like its predecessor, it was a total war. Like its predecessor, it finally led to the defeat of Germany.

What did it add of its own? More. It had the largest armies ever mustered; the biggest battles ever waged; the most troops ever captured; the widest range of ages; and the most significant number of women ever militarily involved. What's more:

- 2,000,000 Germans invaded Russia on June 22, 1941;
- 6,000 Russian tanks were committed to the battle of Kursk-Opel in 1943;
- 425,000 women served in the British military forces;
- 800,000 Russian women served on the eastern front;
- Both 16-year-old boys and 60-year-old men served in the German *Volkssturm*, or home guard, in 1945.

Militarily, World War II was the opposite of World War I. Aside from a number of sieges (the city of Leningrad endured a Nazi siege for 506 days, the longest in modern history), the war moved swiftly on wide fronts. Effective use of modern industrial transportation—bombers and tanks, fighter planes and troop carriers—all gave greater mobility to the fighting forces. Yet the war in Europe remained one chiefly fought by the infantry, supported by aircraft and motorized vehicles.

A COGENT MILITARY ANALYSIS OF THE PHASES OF WORLD WAR II IN EUROPE

Germans in, Germans out.

The former went by fairly quickly; the latter seemed to take forever.

THE TAME, TAME WEST

After the rapid defeat of Poland, everyone braced for a monster battle in western Europe. However, for about nine months nothing much happened there, a nonevent known as the "phoney war." The Germans did manage a field trip up north in April 1940 to bring Denmark and Norway under their control. But the anticipated attack against France was delayed, principally by weather. It wasn't until May 10 that the Germans unleashed their forces against the Netherlands, Belgium, and France. In six weeks, Belgium and the Netherlands were overrun and France was defeated. The daring of the Germans, the more effective use of their equipment (the French did actually have better tanks), the dispirited nature of the French army and population, all contributed to German victory. As France staggered militarily, Mussolini jumped into the war on June 11 and did his best to kick the French while they were down. The French, however, did some kicking of their own, repelling the Italian troops in the southeast.

But there was no doubting the disaster of France's rapid fall. It was so quick that the Germans trapped the British forces at the port of Dunkirk. Seeing its troops' backs to the sea and hopelessly outnumbered, England dispatched everything that could float—from schooners to rowboats—across the channel in a desperate rescue operation. In a spectacular moment, the operation evacuated over 215,000 British and 120,000 French from Dunkirk.

If Dunkirk bothered Hitler, he didn't show it; he had too much to celebrate. In June he required the French to sign an armistice in the same railroad car in which the Germans had been forced to sign the Armistice of 1918. The armistice provided for the division of France into a German-occupied north and an unoccupied south under a pro-German government headquartered in the city of Vichy. Never light on his feet, Hitler was seen in a pose that suggested—but was not—a little jig done just after the document was signed.

With France cowed, Hitler turned to England, who now faced the Nazi war machine alone. While the Nazis had plans for a naval invasion of the British Isles ("Operation Sea Lion"), they were hesitant to execute the plan, let alone amass the necessary equipment. Whatever the details of the plan, it was sure to prove a huge expense. Hermann Goering, com-

Darkness falls on the City of Light:
Hitler in Paris after the signing of the armistice.

mander of the German *Luftwaffe* (air force), his expanding waist rapidly overtaking his ever-inflated self-worth, convinced Hitler to let him use the *Luftwaffe* to bring the English to their knees. Perhaps the island would sue for peace after some relentless bombing. Hitler agreed, and the Battle of Britain began.

Goering sent his bombers—Henkels, Dorniers, Wolff-Schmidts, and Junkers—by the hundreds, in nightly raid after nightly raid. They bombed factories and cities, killed soldiers and civilians. Every night brought a nationwide blackout and the dreaded wait until the drone of German bombers announced the

BOMBS AWAY

During the First World War, aircraft were used primarily for scouting enemy positions. Bombing was notoriously inefficient. Dropping a bomb was like dropping a water balloon—you just hung it over the side of the plane and closed one eye. (It wasn't until the middle of the war that you could even fire a machine gun from a plane without the risk of hitting your own propeller.) By the end of the war, though, it was clear that aerial bombing was an idea whose time had come.

World War II was that time. From the London Blitz to the Dresden firestorm, bombing rained destruction throughout Europe. Late in the war, the Germans came up with a bomber that didn't even need a pilot. It was called the V-1, and known as the "buzz bomb," but what it *should* have been called was a missile.

imminent bombing. Relentless it was, and ruthless, but the English—too obstinate to know that they were defeated—fought on.

The English had several major weapons at their disposal: radar, by which they could detect German aerial movement; excellent fighter aircraft in the form of Spitfires and Hurricanes; and the rhetoric of Winston Churchill. The last was very important, especially during the lengthy London Blitz. The *Luftwaffe's* incessant raids were designed primarily to break English morale and destroy their willingness to continue the war. But Churchill captured the spirit of the English people and expressed it with almost poetic measure, refusing to even acknowledge the possibility of defeat. England weathered the Nazi worst and gave back in kind, as British fighters took a heavy toll on German bombers. By the autumn of 1940, the Battle of Britain had ended; England was bloody but unbowed.

Hitler turned his attention back to the Continent to rescue the Italians from an ill-begotten war. Mussolini, after having been stung by the French, had gone to war against the Greeks—and proceeded to get trounced again. So poorly did the Italians fight that they had to retreat to Albania, which they had annexed in 1939. In the spring of 1941, the Germans invaded the Balkans and even undertook a spectacular and costly parachute drop on Crete to assist Mussolini.

"Il Dunce" continued his quest for punishment with a 1940 invasion of British-occupied Egypt, launched from the Italian colony of Libya. By December the English had taken 130,000 Italian prisoners of war. In February, Hitler sent General Erwin Rommel

AND NOW FOR THE WORLD WAR II ALL-STARS:

For the *Axis Powers* (so-called because a 1936 agreement between Germany and Italy was expected to be the axis—or axle—around which all Europe would revolve): Germany, Italy and Japan, in 1939, followed by Bulgaria, Hungary, and Romania in 1941.

For the *Allied Forces:* Great Britain and France, in 1939; followed by Russia and the United States in 1941. (There were, of course, other participants in the allied cause—more than 40, in fact—but these four were the major players.)

to North Africa with a large contingent called the *Afrika Korps.* Rommel's brilliance at desert warfare earned him promotion to field marshal as well as the nickname "the Desert Fox." By the late spring of 1941, his troops and tanks were at the border of Egypt—within shouting distance of the strategically vital Suez Canal, held by the British. However, he got no farther. Hitler's attention turned to "Operation Barbarossa," his plan for the invasion of the Soviet Union. Supplies and troops were diverted to the forthcoming operation. Rommel burned at having been relegated to fighting a holding action, but Hitler saw his destiny fulfilled to the east. He intended to exterminate the hated communists, enslave the Soviet people, and exploit Russia to feed the people of the Third Reich. If Barbarossa succeeded, it would mean nothing less than mass murder by starvation, forced labor, or execution.

It was the very same program the Nazis had planned for the Jews.

ALL QUIET ON THE EASTERN SET!

You may have seen the movies *The Guns of Navarone* or *Where Eagles Dare,* fictional stories about daring World War II adventures. Herewith, three true stories which might have made better films:

Norsk by Northwest: On a moonlit February night in 1943 six Norwegians, trained as Special Forces men by the British army, parachute into German occupied Norway. Their mission: cripple the heavy-water plant at Vemork, reportedly being used by the Nazis in the development of their own atomic weapon. Wearing white suits that blend into the snow, carrying cyanide capsules in the event of capture, they slip past German sentries, plant their explosives, and slip back out. Minutes later the plant is disabled.

Flight of Fancy: In 1941, Rudolf Hess—second in line to succeed Hitler (after Field Marshal Hermann Goering), the man who helped transcribe *Mein Kampf* while in prison with its author, Adolf Hitler makes a secret solo flight across the English Channel. Parachuting into Scotland, he announces that he has come to negotiate peace between England and Nazi Germany. A furious Hitler disowns his former friend, and orders him to be shot on sight; the English conclude that Hess is mentally disturbed. After the war, Hess is found guilty of war crimes, and sentenced to life imprisonment. Held at Spandau prison after 1945,

ALL QUIET ON THE EASTERN SET!
(*continued*)
. . . .
for 21 years (1966–1987) he is its sole inmate until he kills himself at 93.

Duce's Wild: In July 1943, Italy's fascist dictator Benito Mussolini is deposed by his former allies and held prisoner at a mountaintop villa. Under orders from Mussolini's fascist pal Adolf Hitler, a team of commandos uses gliders to swoop in and rescue the Duce. Using German troops, Hitler restores Mussolini as head of a fascist state in northern Italy. All's well that ends well in 1945, as this head of a puppet state becomes a marionette when his own countrymen string him up.

HOLOCAUST

Virulent anti-Semitism, a cornerstone of Nazi philosophy and policy, reached its horrifying extreme during the war. Upon taking power in 1933, Hitler had embarked on a program of systematic, State-sanctioned persecution of German Jews—depriving them of citizenship, boycotting or simply seizing their businesses, forbidding them to own property. This persecution was part of a Nazi campaign to rid the Third Reich of its racial and moral "undesirables," a process known as Aryanization. All Jews, as well as gypsies, homosexuals, and people with mental or physical disabilities were to be swept from German society—through harassment, detentive custody, or forced emigration—

in order to make room for "pure," Aryan Germans. Hitler's eventual plan for the Jews, however, wasn't simply dispossession, humiliation, and removal from German society—but the extermination of Europe's entire Jewish population.

War gave him the means to accomplish his goal. As the German army seized territory, special units would separate Jews from the rest of the occupied population, walling them up in ghettos (as in Warsaw), sending them to detention camps, or simply executing them on the spot. (In 1941, over 33,000 Soviet Jews would be executed over two days at Babi Yar, in the Ukraine.)

In the summer of 1941, Gestapo chief Reinhard Heydrich (1900–1945) was given the responsibility of formulating the "final solution to the Jewish question." That the solution entailed genocide was already understood. Heydrich's job was to put together an organization dedicated to the task. Under his direction, Germany's architects, railroad workers, engineers, and heads of industry dedicated their energies to making the extermination of the Jews as efficient as possible, competing to provide the Reich with the special rail lines, gas crystals and chambers, and crematoria needed to handle the human traffic. Death camps ringed with barbed wire, machine-gun towers, and searchlights were constructed—islands of despair whose names are a testament to the horrors of what would come to be called the Holocaust: Auschwitz, Dachau, Sobibor, Buchenwald, Bergen-Belsen, Treblinka.

Brought to camps in crowded freight cars and sorted by method of extermination, whole families were torn apart and sent to their deaths. The able-bodied were packed away in barracks to provide slave labor until exhaustion, starvation, or disease claimed them. Those too young, old, weak, or infirm to work were stripped of clothing and valuables, then herded into gas chambers by the hundreds. Many were subjected to medical experimentation before being killed. In Auschwitz, now the most infamous of these camps, the Nazis would kill some 6,000 people a day in 1944.

No expression of outrage could match the stark horror of the numbers. By war's end, 6 million Jews had gone to their deaths at the hands of the Nazis.

DON'T MESS WITH MOTHER RUSSIA

Having secured Western Europe and the Balkans by the summer of 1941, Hitler looked toward Russia. Where Napoleon had failed, Hitler would succeed—or so the Führer thought. On June 22, 1941, he launched the largest military invasion of all time. Some 2 million men and 2,000 tanks rolled eastward, meeting little resistance because the Soviet leadership, despite signs of the impending invasion, had trusted in their mutual nonaggression pact with the Germans.

Barbarossa came very near to success. In the end it failed before the same weapons that had crushed the French emperor: Russia's sheer immensity, the brutality of its winter, and the unbreakable will of the Russian people.

Despite the unimpeded onward rush of the Germans, Stalin literally had enough space to prepare the

defense of the key cities of Moscow and Leningrad.
The further the Germans penetrated, the more their
supply lines extended, until they stretched to the

*Hitler visits Napoleon's tomb but apparently
fails to learn from its history:
Hitler's armies would soon retrace Napoleon's
disastrous route into Russia—and back.*

breaking point. What broke them was the Russian winter. First heavy rain, then heavy snow fell in October, denying Hitler the additional month of good weather he needed for victory. The unprepared German soldiers shivered in summer uniforms; German equipment bogged down; engines froze. The Germans' advance slowed.

The turning point of the war was the battle of Stalingrad. The Germans had besieged the city in the winter of 1941–1942, but now, in the autumn of 1942, they were determined to take it. In some of the most ruthless fighting of the war, Germans and Russians fought street to street, house to house, for the possession of Stalingrad. In the meantime, the Soviet army undertook a careful encirclement of the city, trapping the German Sixth Army under General Paulus. The Sixth Army, a force of 500,000 men that had slugged its way into the center of Stalingrad, faced annihilation unless it retreated. But Hitler refused to allow Paulus to surrender an inch of territory.

Faced with a devastating winter, unable to get supplies, and now unable to retreat, Paulus saw no solution but surrender. Hitler, in a histrionic historical act, suddenly promoted Paulus to the rank of field marshal, taking care to remind Paulus that no German field marshal had ever surrendered. Paulus followed the dictates of duty—to his men, that is. In early 1943 he surrendered, as did 80,000 of his soldiers—all that remained of the half million who had burst into Russia. In Berlin, after a brief announcement informed the German people of the German army's first major defeat, propaganda minister Josef Goebbels ordered

*This map, from a contemporary
American newspaper, shows
the German invasion of the
Soviet Union on June 22, 1941.*

Beethoven's Fifth Symphony to be played on the radio system. The Ninth Symphony's "Ode to Joy" seemed somehow inappropriate.

"Say Uncle . . ." Sam

On December 7, 1941, the Germans got some good news and some bad news from Japan, with whom both Italy and Germany had signed a 1940 mutual assistance pact. The good news was that Japan had carried out a bold and brilliant surprise attack. The bad news was that they had attacked the United States. Germany and Italy were obligated to declare war on the United States, and did so on December 10, 1941.

The first indication that American entry was going to make a difference was the invasion of North Africa by an essentially American force on November 8, 1942. By then, the British, under General Bernard Montgomery, had pushed Rommel and his *Afrika Korps* back to Tunisia. By March of 1943, the combined strength of Americans and British brought the surrender of the Italians and Germans. Rommel, however, was not personally among them. Rommel had returned to Germany to lead the defense of German-occupied Europe.

The Germans were being squeezed by the combination of Allied forces. The Russians had launched an extended counter-offensive, slowly pushing the Germans back to the west. In the meantime, on July 10, 1943, the Allies began an invasion of Italy with landings on Sicily. Barely two weeks had passed when Mus-

THE BOMB
. . . .

The surrender of Germany on April 6, 1945 left Imperial Japan alone against the might of the Allies. The island nation had initially joined Germany and Italy in the Tripartite Pact of 1940—a recognition of their mutual hunger for territory, hostility towards Communism, militaristic rule, and inability to get along with the neighbors.

After Germany and Italy surrendered, Japan—although clearly unable to win the war on its own—showed no disposition towards acceding to the Allies' demand for unconditional surrender. The Allies were forced to close in on Japan island by island, mile by mile, down to the last Japanese soldier. In the face of such ferocity, frustrated by Janpan's insistence on a conditional surrender, U.S. President Harry Truman decided to make use of a new and terrible weapon—the atomic bomb. His rationale for dropping the bomb was "to shorten the agony of war," thus saving the lives of American soldiers; yet other less noble factors played their part: justifying the huge expenditure in developing the bomb; demonstrating American might before Stalin; exacting revence on the Japanese for their treachery at Pearl Harbor.

On August 6, 1945, the U.S. B-29 bomber *Enola Gay* exploded the atomic bomb over Hiroshima; hours later Truman announced that "we shall continue to use it until we completely destroy Japan's power to make war." Three days later he ordered a second atomic bomb exploded over the city of Nagasaki. On August 14, the Japanese surrendered.

THE BOMB (*continued*)

Ironically, the development of the atomic bomb owed a great deal to Germany's Albert Einstein, Italy's Enrico Fermi, Hungary's Leo Szilard, and Denmark's Niels Bohr—physicists who, having fled the totalitarian regimes of Japan's erstwhile partners, all contributed to the American effort to build the bomb.

solini was forced from power. As usual, Hitler tried to bail out his fascist friend by rushing troops in, and a bitter peninsular war lasted even after the Allies' liberation of a jubilant Rome on June 4, 1944—two days before an even more liberating event.

On June 6, 1944, Allied forces landed at Normandy, on the coast of France, in the largest amphibious operation ever undertaken. So memorable was it that the generic military designation used to mark the day of *any* operation—D-Day—has come to stand for this one particular event. Marked by overwhelming numbers of infantry and staggering losses, the invasion, code-named "Overlord," seemed initially precarious but soon succeeded. The Allies forced the Germans back, just as the Russians were doing from the east. For the remaining months of the war, the Germans essentially fought rearguard actions until little was left of the nation's territory. By the middle of April 1945, the Russians were in Berlin.

Mussolini and Hitler left the world sordidly. Mussolini, briefly made head of a minor northern Italian state by the Germans, was captured and shot in the last days of the war. Both his body and that of his mistress were strung up by the feet from the roof of a Milan gasoline station, where a crowd used them as piñatas. Hitler, deep in a Berlin bunker underneath the Chancellery Building, bade farewell to his remaining few associates on April 30. With his new wife, Eva Braun, he committed suicide on April 30, 1945. She took poison; he shot himself in the mouth.

*On February 13, 1945, Allied bombers blanketed Dresden—
a city with no strategic importance—with incendiaries,
to retaliate for the German bombing of England,
to demonstrate the brutal resolve of the Allies, and
to break German morale. The ensuing firestorm took
135,000 lives. (Immediate casualties at Hiroshima,
seven months later, would number 130,000.)*

The war in Europe ended in the unconditional surrender of the Germans on May 7, 1945—V-E Day. Just as significant a date for the future of the Continent was August 6, 1945, when the United States exploded the atomic bomb over Hiroshima, Japan. Hiroshima signaled the beginning of the Nuclear Age that—

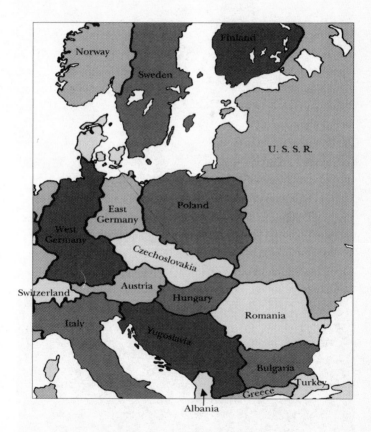

*Post WWII Europe, 1945: The Iron Curtain
falls on the European Theater*

*On August 6, 1945, one bomb destroyed one city,
and changed the lives of billions forever.*

with the successful test of the Soviet's first atomic bomb four years later—would replace the phrase "balance of power" with "balance of terror."

WORLD WAR 2, GERMANY 0

With the end of hostilities, the United States, England, and the Soviet Union (known as "the Big Three," a refreshing change from phrases like Triple Entente and Quadruple Alliance) implemented the plans for postwar Europe that they had been formulating since late 1943.

Until such time as the Germans could come up with a government uninterested in world conquest, Germany was divided into four zones of occupation, each zone under the military administration of either the United States, Great Britain, the Soviet Union, or France. (Liberated from Nazi occupation, France was now back in business under General Charles de Gaulle (1890–1970), who in exile had led French resistance against the Germans.) The German capital of Berlin, situated in the Russian-occupied zone, was partitioned in the same manner. Military occupation meant that the winners didn't have to wait for the Germans to come up with cash war reparations. They could simply take goods and services from their respective zones.

The Big Three also established a four-power tribunal in Nuremberg to try Germany's leaders for war crimes. They also outlawed the Nazi Party—an order that may have been unnecessary, since there was apparently no longer anyone in Germany who would admit to being a Nazi anyway.

PROMISES, PROMISES
. . . .

In order to coordinate their war aims, the soon-to-be victorious United States, Soviet Union, and Great Britain held a series of summits. Along with deciding such matters as the D-Day invasion, the leaders made the following decisions:

- At Teheran in November 1943, Franklin D. Roosevelt, Joseph Stalin, and Winston Churchill agreed that their countries would be pals after the war.

- At Yalta in February 1945, the same three agreed that countries liberated from Nazi rule would be able to form their own democratically elected government.

Would you buy a used continent from these men?

PROMISES, PROMISES (*continued*)

•At Potsdam in August 1945, Stalin, Churchill, and President Truman (Roosevelt had died in April) agreed to encourage democracy in their respective zones of occupied Germany.

Looks like *somebody* had his fingers crossed.

As for the rest of Europe, the postwar plan restored prewar political entities. In 1945 Austria was separated from Germany and given the four-power occupation treatment; Poland was reconstituted, its borders somewhat changed (in return for ceding territory in the east to the USSR, the Poles gained ground in the west, courtesy of the Germans); Czechoslovakia was restored as an independent nation.

Finally, an international organization was established to promote security and cooperation—the United Nations. (No one much cared for "League of Nations: The Return.") As early as August 1941, Winston Churchill and FDR had signed the Atlantic Charter, a rather hopeful declaration that once Hitler had been beaten, the rest of the world could live in peace and harmony without ever again resorting to violence. This philosophy was so obviously benevolent, and so obviously unrealistic, that almost everyone on earth endorsed it (except Hitler, who took exception to the bit about getting beaten). In October of 1945, fifty-one member nations put the Atlantic Charter's principles into practice with an agreement establishing the

United Nations. Its mission, in part, was to maintain international stability and cooperation among nations.

But it soon became clear that cooperation was the last thing on the minds of its two most powerful members—the United States and the Soviet Union.

COLD WAR

Like many wartime marriages, the alliance between the Western powers and the Soviet Union failed to survive the peace. With Germany out of the way, it was obvious that there were only two major players left in the power game, one at each end of the political spectrum—the democratic United States and the communist Soviet Union. Everyone else had gone bust: France ravaged by years of occupation; Great Britain exhausted by its Herculean effort; Italy and Germany battle-scarred and beaten. In the strategic vacuum following the German surrender, both the United States and the USSR saw an opportunity to strengthen its hand at the expense of the other. The ensuing struggle for European domination split Germany in two, polarized the Continent, and began a fierce competition for the hearts and minds of the world.

Between 1945 and 1948 the Soviet Union, through military intimidation and political subterfuge, saw to it that communist regimes were established throughout Eastern Europe. Poland, Bulgaria, Hungary, Romania, Albania, Yugoslavia, and Czechoslovakia all fell under Soviet influence, severing their economic, political, social, and military ties to the West. The subsequent isolation of Eastern Europe prompted Winston Churchill, in a 1946 speech, to remark that "an iron curtain has descended across the Continent."

In response, the United States used the power of the dollar to shore up democracy in the western end of Europe. The Marshall Plan, named after U.S. Secretary of State George Marshall (1880–1959) and carried out from 1947 to 1952 under President Truman, offered huge loans to European nations struggling to rebuild their economies—provided, of course, that they embraced democratic principles.

Germany, occupied by both communist and democratic forces, was torn apart. Both the United States and the USSR recognized that even a defeated and devastated Germany could eventually be rebuilt into a military-industrial power. The Soviet Union wouldn't hear of an independent, strong, democratic Germany; they had to ensure that never again would a German army—imperial, fascist, *or* capitalist—begin marching on Moscow. The best way to achieve that would be to turn Germany into a communist satellite.

The United States feared that a Soviet-dominated Germany would lead to communist control of Europe. They needed a democratic, economically renewed German Republic to provide a bulwark against Soviet expansion.

Both got what they wanted. In 1948 the USSR withdrew its participation in the Allied occupation of Germany, establishing communist rule in the Soviet-occupied zone of eastern Germany. In response, the United States, Great Britain, and France combined their occupied territory in 1949 to form the Federal

A CITY HELD HOSTAGE

One of the earliest and most significant battles of the Cold War took place in Berlin. The German capital, divided like the rest of the country into American, British, French, and Russian zones of occupation, lay deep within Soviet-occupied Germany. On June 24, 1948, the Soviets closed all ground routes into the western zones of the city, hoping to starve the West Berliners into turning against the French, British, and U.S. occupation forces.

The West Berliners, far from surrendering to this Soviet extortion, made it clear they would undergo any hardship to keep the Soviets from taking the entire city. The western allies responded to this loyalty with an eleven-month airlift that, in over 200,000 flights, delivered over 2 million tons of goods to their

The Berlin Wall, built in 1961 to stem the tide of East German refugees into West Berlin and freedom, would stand for 28 years as a cruel monument to Cold War.

A CITY HELD HOSTAGE (*continued*)

sections of Berlin. (At one point, planes were landing at the rate of one every two minutes.)

On May 12, 1949, the Soviets gave up. The blockade ended, leaving two unexpected accomplishments: the forging of friendship and respect between the western allies and their former enemies, the Germans; and an important public relations coup for democracy. A monument commemorating the airlift was erected at Berlin's Tempelhof Airport. (To commemorate *their* relationship with the people of Berlin, the Soviets erected a monument of their own in 1961— the Berlin Wall, built to keep East Berliners from leaving.)

Republic of Germany. This was answered by the Soviet's official creation of the German Democratic Republic later that year. Once the common enemy of both communism and democracy, Germany had become the symbol of their mutual enmity.

The battle lines were now drawn for a new kind of conflict, one fought by every means except military: the Cold War. Europe had become the arena in which two superpowers struggled for world domination. The Continental balance of power, once an intricate system of alliances, ententes, and state systems, had become part of a global shirts-and-skins game. You either played for the United States or the Soviet Union; it was a very small league.

Two world wars had stripped Europe of its preeminence. Global domination had passed to the

United States and Russia—the former, a cordial but distressingly independent relative; the latter, a former member who had not only outgrown the European club but also was threatening to dissolve it. In 1945, with its empires crumbling, its financial health ruined, and its military strength exhausted, Europe found itself without an identity. In the decades to follow, European nations would have to redefine their roles as players, not playmakers.

It would be a familiar task; Europe has always struggled to define itself. Unlike other continents, Europe's very boundaries often seem more a matter of convenience than anything else. Great Britain has always made the most of the twenty-one-mile-wide strip of water (at its narrowest point) that separates it from the continent—acting at times as if the English Channel were the size of the Atlantic; at other times, as if it could be crossed in a single step. Russia's membership in Europe has always been a matter of choice, not necessity. The Balkans have been victims in an East-West tug-of-war for hundreds of years. Europe's central territory, curiously enough, has always been the most disjointed, from the decentralized Holy Roman Empire to the fall of the Third Reich; even today's re-unified Germany is but a few years old.

After the tumult of the seventeenth century, it was obvious that Europe could define itself neither as a Christian monolith nor as the imperial territory of a single dynastic family. Instead, the Continent resolved itself into a balance of continually shifting forces: economic, political, and military power controlled through coalition, alliance, and congress. As national entities changed, Europe flexed and adapted, attempting to maintain a state of equilibrium—yet always with the sense that it was in the forefront. Europe's revolutionaries believed their cause would unite the world; its capitalists believed theirs would enrich it; its moralists that theirs would liberate it. Leading the field industrially, economically, and militarily, Europe never seemed to think there might be a point at which the rest of the world would simply catch up—let alone pass it.

Yet even in relinquishing its role as leader, Europe remained in the vanguard. As the Soviet Union collapsed under its own weight, leaving the United States without its worse half, the two postwar titans were left with a question Europe had been facing for centuries: Who are we now?

SUMMARY

The first half of the twentieth century was an age of two world wars (1914–1918 and 1939–1945) divided by an interlude, during which everyone got ready for the next war.

Dictatorships of right and left (Nazi, Fascist, and Communist) emerged from World War I and the Great Depression, quickly combining all institutions into a police state.

The two world wars devastated Europe, encouraged the dissolution of its colonial empires, and ended the Continent's domination of world affairs.

The Nuclear Age began as the two global superpowers—the United States and the Soviet Union—faced off in a Cold War.

ABOUT THE
AUTHOR

Although writing has been ROBERT P. LIBBON's first
love, it has rarely been his sole career. For thirteen
years he served as Production Manager and Performance Director for New York's Big Apple Circus. After
leaving the circus, he spent four years as "Director of
Covert Activities" for the magicians Penn & Teller.
Libbon lives in New York City with his wife, Janet, and
their two cats, Vera and Rosie.